THE KINGDOM HALL NO MORE

Daniel J. Chamberlayne

authorHOUSE®

AuthorHouse™
1663 Liberty Drive, Suite 200
Bloomington, IN 47403
www.authorhouse.com
Phone: 1-800-839-8640

First published by AuthorHouse 9/4/2008

ISBN: 978-1-4343-9698-3 (e)
ISBN: 978-1-4343-9697-6 (sc)
ISBN: 978-1-4343-9695-2 (hc)

Printed in the United States of America
Bloomington, Indiana

This book is printed on acid-free paper.

Editing: DaChosen Publishing and CNG Publishing
Research: Daniel Chamberlayne
Web sites:
www.myspace.com/kingdomhallnomore

This book is dedicated to...

My father, Warren Chamberlayne,
Who is no longer here in the
Physical but has never left me.
I love you. This one is for you

To my Mother, Louise Chamberlayne,
I know you raised me the best way
That you knew how. In the bible there is a scripture
That says to honor thy mother and father
And that's all I always wanted to do.
Without you, this book wouldn't be possible.

I love you,
Daniel

The Kingdom Hall... No More!

TABLE OF CONTENTS

ACKNOWLEDGMENTS

First and Foremost, I would like to acknowledge GOD for blessing my family and me because without him, this book wouldn't be possible. I owe a great deal to my wife, Kim, who gave me the inspiration to write such a book about my difficult and sometimes sad upbringing. She had to endure many long nights alone while I was in our computer room typing all night and putting everything that I remembered on paper. Finally after 10 years, my dream has been accomplished and is now a reality. Thank you, Kim, for having my back on this. I want to thank my son, little Daniel for asking me everyday if my book was done yet. I want to thank my sisters, Denise and Greta, for taking the time to read some of the chapters to verify some incidents that I mentioned. I must give a shout out Tracey Wing field for introducing me into publishing business.

I must thank some of my childhood friends that went to the Kingdom Hall with me while we were growing up. Shout out to my friends Tim and Joe and my homeboy Kendo. We are always reminiscing our childhood and the times we all shared growing up in "the truth". I must thank my Aunt Laura, who discussed countless stories of my childhood with me and who I always have a great time talking on the phone with all night. I thank her children Champ, Moses, Melissa, Laura and their kids as well. I want to thank my Uncles Francis and Uncle Edwin and their wives for providing me with some additional information about my father that I didn't remember. I must thank one of my best friends Keith Richardson for being there when everyone else wasn't and believing that I could do anything I wanted. I want to thank my man, James Apple White from the website MEDIABRUNCH.com, and Shawn from the website JWFILES.com. I want to give a big shout out to some families I grew up with: The Benjamin family, The George family, the Young family, the Jacobs Family, the Richardson family, my Aunt Sattie in the Bronx, Matt Boser, who called me his son. I want to acknowledge my friend Sandra from Freeport. Shout out to all my childhood peoples who I grew up with that lived off of Farmers Blvd, Murdock Avenue, Liberty Avenue, and Linden Blvd. All my peoples from the park, the rock on Farmers Blvd, all my peoples from my first job (First Boston at the World Trade Center), Lazard Freres, Cunard Cruise LTD, Kramer Levin in New York. I want to give props to all my peoples that grew up with me that lived on Farmers Blvd and 112th Rd. I want to give a huge shout out to LL Cool J and Mikey D (two of the nicest emcees I ever heard rhyme). I want to give thanks to the entire 90.3 WBAU Radio Crew from Adelphi University. All my disc jockeys who used to DJ or make beats for me, Doctor Dre from YO MTV Raps (NY radio) who invited me up to the radio station, Ed lover from Hollis, Queens, Run-DMC, Public Enemy, MC DJ Flavor, I owe you one, Bob and the Mob from Hollis, FUBU, DJ Cut Creator, My man Troy L from Harlem, My childhood friend Jeff Sanders from the R&B group INTRO, Afrika Bambaataa and the Almighty Universal Zulu Nation, DJ Jazzy Jay, my entire New York peoples that relocated to Atlanta, Georgia. I want to thank Randle Battle and Double Exposure in New York for their assistance of this book, Saundra Barnes and her family for networking, I want to acknowledge all the internet magazines and radio websites that reached out to me and interviewed me. Big shout outs to all my friends on MYSPACE and BLACKPLANET that I've met and supported me through out the writing of this book. I want to acknowledge all my childhood peoples that used to attend the Kingdom Hall that have died, or have gotten disfellowshipped, disassociated, or just left. I also want to thank my cousins Jesse and Helena Giddens in California for spiritual inspiration. I want to acknowledge New Birth and New Mercies and their Senior Pastors for showing my family and I love. I want to thank my other cousins Troy and Sandy Berger and family, The Younger Family, The Chamberlayne family, The Michael family, The Daniels Family, Schuyler Michael and his family, my Uncle Earl and his family, my Uncle Junior (the coolest man EVER) and his family. And finally, shout out to my nephews and nieces and cousins

The Kingdom Hall… No More!

KINGDOM HALL BUZZ WORDS AND PHRASES

The Truth	The Society
Present Truth	The Organization
Accurate Knowledge	WTBTS
Kingdom Interests	The True Organization
Loyalty to Jehovah	The Only True Religion
Where else is there to go?	Jehovah's Organization
Good news of the Kingdom	Jehovah's Chosen Organization
The Prize	Jehovah's People
Righteousness	YHWH
Undeserved Kindness	The New System
Spiritual	Paradise
Sheeplike ones	Kingdom
Brotherhood	The New Order
The Friends	Theocratic Order
Theocratic	The Flock
Agape	The Lord's People
Meat in Due Season	Fold
Pure Language	God's Channel
Consecrated	Faithful and Discreet Slave
Worship Jehovah	Governing Body
Jehovah's Theocratic Arrangement	144,000
Loyalty	Anointed
Those Taking the Lead	Bethel
Paradise Earth	The Farm
New System of Things	Gilead
The New System	Brooklyn

The New Order	Great Crowd
Meek Ones will possess the earth	True Christians
Righteous New Order	Faithful Christians
Worldwide Preaching	District Overseer
Preaching Work	Circuit Overseer
Service	The Body of Elders
Field Service	Elders
Field Service Time	Book Study Overseer
Informal Witnessing	Ministerial Servants
Street-work	Brothers
Voluntary Donations	Sisters
Subscription	Pioneers
Ministry	Special Pioneers
Preaching	Auxiliary Pioneers
Door to Door	The JWs
Return Visits	The Remnant
Worldwide Publishing	The Little Flock
Territory	Publisher
In The Original Greek	The Witnesses
Congregation	Bible Students
Kingdom Hall	Us against the World
The Meeting	Persecution
The Service Meeting	Test
Theocratic Ministry School	Waiting on Jehovah
Kingdom Ministry School	New Light
Watchtower Study	Light gets Brighter and Brighter
The Book Study	Adjustments were Made
Public Talk	They are just Imperfect Men
Talk(s)	They make Mistakes
Kingdom Ministry	They Admitted their Mistakes

School	Revealed truth
Second School	Leave it in Jehovah's hands
Householder	Invisible Return
Meeting Attendance	607 BCE
District Convention	1914
District Assembly	King of The North
Circuit Assembly	King of The South
Assembly	Daniel's Prophecy
Convention	The sanctity of blood
Quick Build	Serving Shoulder to Shoulder
Theocratic Library	Shepherding Calls
Literature	Wholeheartedly
Tracts	Meek
Watchtower	Zeal
Awake	Shepherding
Magazines	Brotherly Love
Books	We don't Pass a Plate
Bookbag	Donation Arrangement
Territory	Volunteer Assignment
Daily text	Contribution
Meeting Clothes	Useful Habits
Practicing True Religion	Endurance
Sheep	The greater (Isaiah, Moses, Daniel, etc., fill-in the blank)
Free Bible Study	Useful Habits
House over House	Good Example
Honest-Hearted-ones	Jehovah's Happy People
Volunteers	Happiest People on Earth
Need is great	Be in subjection to your husbands
Unity	Food at the proper time

Admittedly	Zealous
In Harmony With	Abraham's Seed
Jehovah's Blessing	Through Jesus' Name
Encouragement	The Anointed Ones
Time of the end	Fleshy
Partaking of the Emblems	Df'd or D'd
All the more so...	Undeserved Loving Kindness

Buzz Words About JWs Who Are Not In Good Standing

Weak in the Truth	Disfellowshipped
Spiritually Weak	Disassociated
Spiritually not Qualified	Public Reproved
Spiritual Fornication	Privately Reproved
They went to the World	DF'd
Left Jehovah	DA'd
Turned to Satan	Committee Meetings
Apostate	Immoral Conduct
Not putting Spiritual Interests First	Materialistic
They miss Meetings	Turned Worldly
Drifting Away	Bad Association
Stumble	Returned to their own Vomit
Independent Thinking	Spiritually Sick
Inactive	Uncooperative
Not heeding the counsel of the Elders	Marked

Buzz Words about the Worldly System

At Armageddon	That's the World for you
The Great Tribulation	World
This System of Things	Worldly
Worldly System	Worldly People
The Last Days	Worldly Associations
Satan's System	Opposers of Jehovah
Satan	Christendom
God's Adversary, Satan the Devil	United Nations
Devil	Babylon the Great
Demons	World Empire of False Religion
Demonized	Harlot
Demonistic	666
Satan and his Demons	The Last Days
Table of the Demons	Bablonish
Goatlike ones	Pagan
Unbeliever	Gehenna
Bad association spoils useful habits	Like the Original Satan
Haughty Ones	Wicked system of things

Buzz Words in Their Literature

This Clearly Shows . . .	Obviously . . .
The Bible plainly says . . .	Logically . . .
Has clearly shown . . .	Justifiably . . .
We have clearly seen . . .	Surly this is reasonable . . .
The evidence shows . . .	We might reasonable assume . . .
The evidence should be clear . . .	Most/Many Scholars . . .
Reasonably, then . . .	Surely then . . .

Thus the facts make clear . . .	Truly . . .
What must one do . . .	Apparently...
Most certainly...	Of course...
Isn't it reasonable to conclude...	Possibly...
Fine examples...	Probably...
Thus, we can see...	.

Introduction

I *was* a member of the Organization known as the "Jehovah's Witness". This is the most controversial and unorthodox Christian religious group ever to appear in the western hemisphere. Their beliefs are often misunderstood and lopsided in regards to mainstream Christianity and their interpretation of the Bible is different than other religions due to the use of the New World Translation of the Holy Scriptures, or what some people call, "the Jehovah Witnesses bible." For over 16 years, I was knocking on people's door in field service, waking them up on Saturday mornings saying my little sermon and attending all the meetings and conventions even when I didn't want to. I wrestled with my mother to change congregations because I always thought our congregation was not appealing enough to my peers at that time and too rigid. I tried to reason with her about using other bibles or different translations for studying and cross-referencing so when we come across "unbelievers, we can have a better chance reasoning with them. The organization that I was involved with for most of my life and had spiritual ties to for my spirituality is now the same organization I can no longer turn to. I felt like I was spiritually set up and railroaded. I was only taught what my mother believed in and thought to be true. Was it that I lacked faith in Jehovah? Or was it that I never believed that this was "the truth" from jump street? Maybe the elders from the congregation that I had known for many years and watched me grow up into manhood were not fond of me because of my mother not being the zealous and obedient servant of Jehovah that they wanted her to be throughout the years. After years of not letting go, over 16 years of having resentment that had built up inside me for not having my name cleared and being worried what people in the organization thought of me, I needed to address this matter through writing, hoping for complete closure to it all.

I'm now a disfellowshipped individual that has gone back into the world. I have been denied any hope for eternal life here on earth, according to my old organization. I'm this "unrepentant" expelled member of the Jehovah's Witnesses that's not going to live on this paradise Earth with the great crowd and I'm considered worse than a non-believer, referred to as a dog that's returned to its own vomit. For me to return, I would have to adjust my thinking and have a change of attitude and show clear evidence of repentance. There is always the idea of being reinstated, which I can formally write a plea to return back to the organization, becoming fully reinstated if evidence of godly works is shown and an attitude adjustment has been made.

I could go back and put on a good front for Jehovah's Theocratic Arrangement and play this spiritual game and ride it out until "The great day of Armageddon"! After all, men can't read hearts, only GOD can. I'm not doing anything now that would be deemed "unspiritual" or "ungodly". I would be just fooling myself. So now you may be asking, "Why subject myself to the ridicule that I'm going to get when this book drops"?

I was tired of having a religion being forced upon me and having to explain and defend this religion. I wasn't being true to it or myself. I was content with just going to the Kingdom Hall but not becoming a Jehovah's Witness. I saw and heard the horror stories about teenagers and young adults getting forced into the organization not having a say about what they wanted and very few options of choice. Not to sound like I didn't want to be saved or that I didn't want to be in God's favor, but after many years of attending the Kingdom Hall and being taught that being a Jehovah's Witness was the true Christian religion, I felt a need to revaluate my spiritual well being and see what was true and what wasn't. I put myself on spiritual vacation for sometime now and finally found some peace within myself, not living my life as a hypocrite. I needed to write for therapy. After many years, I need mental and emotional closure on 16 years of Jehovah's Witness doctrines that I didn't always agree with. I can recall the horror stories of my peers that grew up with me in the Kingdom Hall. Things never turned out well for them mentally, and they haven't been the same since. They are now spiritually damaged. You the reader might know someone personally that went through what I went through. These people may have even been written off as mentally and spiritually incompetent. It may have barred their success and happiness in life. Some of these kids had fathers that were ELDERS. The Elders are men of the congregation who lead and discipline, watching over the 'flock' or congregation. These Elders had to lead by example, a strict discipline for their own families. How could the Elders be put into these positions and not have their own families straight? What kind of example is that? So a lot of my peers HAD NO CHOICE but to be forced to walk a straight path. Their fathers had been put in high positions as Elders to lead and show by example. Those Elders weren't going to lose their position because their children weren't obedient and not choosing "Jehovah ways." You were either going to conform or be kicked out the house. Most of my peers just couldn't handle it. They either submitted and became a full Jehovah's Witness or became subjected to living homeless and becoming drug addicts, suicidal and mentally unstable. They probably walk around right now with a feeling of uncertainty. Some were blessed and were able to move in with their "worldly friends". Some moved into the house of a "non-believer" relative. The first reaction of any non-believer (especially a relative) is "How can parents do this to you?" I'm talking about the average working teenager. A working teenager who is doing well in school and not on drugs, not getting drunk, not getting arrested and not giving their parents a headache. They just don't want to be a Jehovah's Witness. And this is what their parents subject them to. I have met some Jehovah's Witness parents recently (they didn't know I was disfellowshipped nor did I mention it to them) and they stated they give their children a choice after their child (or children) turns 18. As long as they are active in school and doing something constructive they can stop attending the

Kingdom Hall, go to college, and pursue whatever they want in life. These parents gave their children a choice to decide what's best for them.

The Organization does not encourage members to pursue a higher education, any type of sports or music careers, or other "secular" or worldly activity. If you do, you will be looked down upon. This type of thinking wasn't allowed in most Jehovah's Witness households. If you decided to pursue other avenues of the world without the consent of your family, you definitely had to do what I had to do: live a DOUBLE LIFE. This was what I had to do; this was how I had to live. So you might ask, "If I could lead a double life, why couldn't the others do the same?" Well, for starters, when you lead a double life, you're not being true to yourself. You also risk the chance of someone from the congregation seeing you and telling your parents (or guardian) that they saw you doing something against the doctrines of the organization; and these doctrines were strict. The possibility of being reported to the Elders for not following the organizations strict bible-based guidelines, and risking being put on "public reproved", were high. "Public Reproved" is a form of discipline and it's usually done to young kids or teenagers that haven't been baptized yet and attending the Kingdom Hall with their parents. It's like a small smack on the hand, a warning less severe then being disfellowshipped. Your name is still read out to the congregation with the Brother announcing, "So-and-so has been put on public reprove. This individual isn't to be spoken to and their participation in field service *and* making comments at the meetings and association is limited. This individual needs to get (him or her self) together spiritually."

I do have to express that as strange as my relationship was with my mother, she allowed me to have some sort of balance. She allowed me to be "half spiritual and half worldly" for most of my teen years. Fortunately for me, she was received in the congregation as a sister that was "weak in the truth" or a babe in the spirit. Dropping dime on me, getting me in trouble with my mother, telling her anything about me wasn't going to put any new stripes on someone. After all, in their eyes she was doing the best she could with a male teenager while still being able to attend the meetings. When I got closer to my 18th birthday, my mom did a spiritual turn around and started to put mad pressure on me and wasn't letting up. She was getting more 'spiritual" or "mature in the truth". She started taking this Jehovah's Witness worship very serious. She tightened her grip on me. Then came the hints. She started asking me "Sweetie, when are you going to start taking the 180 questions and get baptized. *YOU KNOW RIGHT FROM WRONG NOW!* Its time for you to start leaning on the fence of Jehovah and not Satan!"

As time went on, my mother damn near pushed me to lean on that fence of Jehovah. A little before my 21st birthday I received a document from my mother to get baptized or leave the home. After reviewing my not-so-few-options, I got baptized. It happened a month after my 21st birthday. Four months later, I stopped going to the Kingdom Hall altogether, and then there was trouble and I was disfellowshipped a year later.

In this book, you will read about my unique situation. You will see how I was able to remain sane. How I handed my situation might be debated among those who read this book. There will be tons of opinions on how my situation could've been handled differently. Through out the book you will discover how much control this organization has over its members. You will see how this organization has affected me spiritually, mentally, and emotionally. I want young adults in particular to read what I had to go through. If they are in a similar situation, and don't know how to handle it because they feel there is no one to turn to, they can read this book. Hopefully, they can relate. Hopefully, you can relate. They can know there is someone else that knows exactly what they are going through. I give warning to those kids: *Don't let the tension build up inside you like it did me; it will only get worse. Start talking to someone! If you are reluctant to talk then WRITE!* I know exactly what you are going through. I know the feelings you are having. It is the feeling of feeling alone. You feel you can't tell your worldly friends because they may not understand anything about the Jehovah's Witness organization. And if you talk to someone in the organization you will be ratted on, and the Elders won't be far behind with a phone call. So that's out. So where and who do you turn to? That's what I said back when I was 20; I felt all those things. I sincerely thought I could put the matter with Jehovah God in prayer. I'm not saying prayer does not work, however, I was taught that Jehovah would answers prayers from people that were in good standing with him and his son Jesus Christ. Not someone like me. That's the only way you are taught to think. That didn't work out. Was there something else I could have done different? The situation plays in the back of my mind over and over. *What could've been? What should I have said?* I still come up empty handed. Deep down in my heart, I know the resolution of the matter came out for the best for all involved. Finally, there is peace within. I continue to search for God because I know there is a loving God that cares.

HERE IS MY STORY.

CHAPTER ONE: NO MORE BIRTHDAY CAKE

It was August 2nd, 1974. I was celebrating my 7th birthday at home with my family. I had a beautiful cake and a good deal of impatience tempting me away from my dinner. But though it was my special day, I had to eat my cold kidney beans before I could have a simple slice of my birthday cake. I wanted my cake, and I wanted to eat it too. When dinner was finally finished, my family did a happy birthday song and I blew out the 7 candles, making a wish, and beginning a wonderful birthday. I didn't realize that this would be my last birthday celebration as a kid. Life was going to change for me drastically in the next coming weeks. I didn't have a clue that my life would change forever. The first of three events would occur on September 1st, 1974. My family was supposed to be in New Jersey with my Uncle (my father's brother) and his family celebrating his birthday. Our families gathered every September 1st to celebrate my Uncle's birthday. But this year, due to my mother studying with Jehovah Witnesses, my mother wanted to go somewhere else. At the last minute, my family was able to get a very inexpensive trip to Acapulco, Mexico. My father received discounts because he worked for Pan Am Airlines as a Jet Mechanic. My family would travel all over the world via standby or employee discount. So, going to Mexico at the last minute wasn't unusual. However, going to Mexico around the time of my Uncle's birthday was odd. Every September 1st had dedicated to celebrating my Uncle's birthday with a trip to New Jersey. My father wouldn't miss his brother's birthday for anything. Our family wouldn't miss it for anything. My mother wanted no more parts of celebrating birthdays, despite celebrating my birthday 4 weeks prior to September 1st. I'm pretty sure she may have suggested to my father to go elsewhere, where there wouldn't be any birthday celebrations going on.

My mother was studying the bible with a Jehovah's Witness lady by the name of Sister Patti who lived near us in St. Albans, Queens, New York. She also arranged for my sister to have a bible study with a lady by the name of Sister Brisler. Sister Patti would pick my mother and sister up from the house and they would attend meetings at the Kingdom Hall on Hollis Avenue and 201st Street in Hollis, Queens, New York. Other times my father would drop my mother and sister off at the Kingdom Hall; and pick them up as well. I stayed with my father. In the beginning it was just my mother and sister going to the Kingdom Hall, not me. My mother would try and get me to come. But my father would say in a stern voice, "No. Daniel is staying with me." That would be the end of the discussion. But my induction into the Kingdom Hall was soon to come.

In the summer of '74, my family and I were in Mexico having a great time. I remember playing in the pool with my father. My father and I were very close, always together. While we were in the pool, my father stated to me that he wanted to go down to the beach. I begged him to stay with me. My sister was in a lounge chair by the pool. I figured it would be okay to hang out with her while my father ventured to the beach. I didn't realize that would be the last time I would see him alive. I fell asleep, and when I woke up alone on the lounge chair, I got nervous. My sister had gone upstairs. The sun was going down and I went looking for my father. I went to the beach; I went to the front of the hotel, to the bar, to the hotel room. I looked *EVERYWHERE*. I checked the pools and nothing. It was getting dark and I was exhausting all possibilities as to where my father could be. Finally, I went back to the hotel room where I saw the hotel manager and hotel doctor talking to my mother. I noticed my mother and sister crying. I asked what happened. I wanted to know what was going on. My mom said through tears, "Your father drowned. The authorities found his body near the beach. Did he tell you he was going to the beach?" I said, "Yes. But I didn't see him go right away. When I last saw

2

him he was near the pool." I still thought that I had heard wrong. I believed he was okay; maybe he had a slight head injury. Maybe he was just a little shook up and we would be going to the hospital to see him recover and then finish our vacation. I was wrong! My mother looked at me and said, "Your father has died and you will never talk to him again." I wasn't going to ever see him again. That day was September 1st, 1974.

My mother had to start making calls back to the states. One call she dreaded making was to my Uncle on where we were supposed to be. September 1st was his birthday. When he and his wife received the call from my mother, they knew something was wrong and some bad news was coming. My uncle accepted the call and heard what happened. He started crying immediately and hasn't been the same since. My father's people always thought there was something wrong and suspicious on how my father died. My father's body was put in a beautiful Mexican casket and his body was flown back to JFK International airport in Queens, NY. Incidentally JFK was also the same airport where my father worked. I received an eerie feeling as we flew in to land at the airport my father worked at. My father used to bring me to his job all the time and now we were bringing his dead body to his job. His memorial service was held at the Kingdom Hall. His funeral was at Gilmore's Funeral parlor on Linden Blvd and 192nd Street in St. Albans, New York. At his funeral, my father's people were very upset. My other uncle from Richmond, VA (also my father's brother) was a little taken back when the US Flag was wrapped and folded (my father was in the Air Force) and given to my mom and then back to him. That was the first incident of many where he noticed how much my mother had changed. The subject about my father's death could be a book on its own. But I choose to leave the subject alone. The only reason I mentioned as much as I did is because if he hadn't passed, I might not be writing this book. Because of his passing, I had to start attending the Kingdom Hall.

3

I remember while my mother was having her bible study, which was from a blue book bound publication called <u>The Truth Book,</u> I was encouraged to have a study session like my sister was having. I started studying this yellow book that had beautiful pictures with kids of different nationalities petting wild animals, playing together in a paradise setting. The name of the book was called <u>The Paradise Book</u>. This was my first real exposure to reading or seeing Kingdom Hall literature. I thought it was a good way to start learning about the bible, through pictures. I was learning lessons on how God created mankind and what role children have. I learned basic bible history. Real easy stuff like Adam and Eve, the serpent in the Garden of Eden, Cain and Abel, the creation of the plants, oceans and seas, the Earth, the land and sea animals, and the names of men and women in the bible and the roles they played. I was learning the names of biblical cities and towns. I was on my way to becoming a young bible pupil and I was looked on as the "new man in the house". This was my mother's way of preparing me for that.

Mourning my father was finally over and my mother decided to move on with her life, taking the next step forward on her spiritual path. She did this by dedicating her life to Jehovah and symbolizing it with her baptism on November 4th, 1974 at the circuit assembly in Washington Heights, Manhattan just outside of Harlem. This was just two months after my father died. One of her closest girlfriends was also baptized that day and they both are still in "the truth" to this day. I didn't have too much of a choice now. I had to start going to the Kingdom Hall on Hollis Avenue and 201st in Hollis, Queens New York. The congregation we attended was called the "Murdock Avenue Congregation". This was the congregation we were assigned to even though our house was in another congregation's territory at that time. Back then the Kingdom Hall on Hollis Avenue had two congregations, which were the Hollis Ave Congregation and the Murdock Ave Congregation. My initial reaction after my first visit to the Hall was that this wasn't a real church. I said that aloud. My mother told me, "You're right. It isn't a church. It's a Kingdom Hall." She said it very proudly. I inspected the place and saw no windows. There were no crosses, no pictures or no images of God or Jesus Christ. I always heard how churches looked inside, but the Kingdom Hall really wasn't a church at all. The things I heard about going on inside a church were the singing and the dancing, the instruments playing, the people clapping and the collection plate being passed. None of that was at the Kingdom Hall. There was singing in the beginning, before an intermission, and at the end of the meeting. But it wasn't like your average Black church. The singing at the Kingdom Hall was dull at best. No Jehovah's Witness were going to be discovered by a record company for a gospel recording anytime soon. The songs were in a pink book. There were 192 songs at that time and they all sounded the same. The usual church lingo or phrases weren't being said at the Kingdom Hall. I had to get used to it all. It was very comfortable, as far as seating. There wasn't a lot of yelling or loud music and there wasn't anyone diving to the floor and catching the Holy Ghost. It wasn't about people yelling out, "Praise the lord" or "Hallelujah" or "Yes, Jesus". There were no outbursts of any kind; instead the kingdom hall was stiff and had a robotic feel. There wasn't a preacher walking back and forth on stage sweating profusely. One of the biggest things the organization loves to tell people who they study the bible with is that *THERE'S NO COLLECTION PLATE BEING PASSED AROUND.* There are contribution boxes through out the Kingdom Hall where a person can contribute any amount they wish. I think the idea of not having a collection plate is the best religious marketing scheme that anyone can come up with. It's very appealing among the organization. They treated my family and me nicely and even had a memorial for my father's passing. I don't think they do that anymore, unless your spouse is 'in the truth'. It was a nice gesture. I really didn't understand what was going on but I knew changes for the worse were approaching.

CHAPTER TWO: 1975

Towards the end of 1974, I remember hearing a lot of talk from my mother and other Jehovah Witnesses about a prophecy, some biblical event that was going to happen in 1975. This prophecy would affect the world, as we knew it. The organization, also known as "the Society", was making references that the "Time of the end" or "Armageddon" was coming; the present world as we knew it was coming to an end. The wicked would be destroyed and Jesus Christ would start his 1,000-year reign. The organization predicted the year 1975 that these events would occur. According to the organization the last days began in the year 1914. The physical facts of our day, such as the First World War, were in fulfillment of prophecy to mark this as the last generation of a wicked world. The organization also had a timetable calculation that man's creation was the year 4026 B.C and six thousand years from man's creation, the world will end. The seventh period of a thousand years of human history would begin in the fall of 1975. God's rest day, the time man has been on earth since creation, and the last generation of this wicked world all ran parallel to 1975. This is what Jehovah God wanted. When my mother tried to explain the 1975 incident I thought it would be something of a World War, a Holy War with angels coming out of the sky and fighting demons. Jesus Christ was going to be shown on TV; Satan would be standing next to the World leaders. It would end with Jehovah killing Satan, the world leaders, and anyone that sided with Satan. I was thinking all the Jehovah's Witnesses would be saved, being united across the earth after the war; all the Jehovah's Witnesses would start helping to clean up the earth. I was envisioning the Elders showing us the blueprints of a paradise earth. New York City would be the first place that a paradise was going to be. My mother stated everything we do in life would change. The organization was saying that Jehovah's

6

Witnesses should be aware of the upcoming world events. We were told not to seek higher education, turn down scholarships and high paying jobs. Elders urged publishers to get into pioneer service for there was a short time left.

Here are some quotes from The Watchtower and the Awake magazines and Tract Society FROM THEIR OWN PUBLICATIONS about what was mentioned for the year of 1975:

Awake, 5/22/69, pg. 15 ✍ "if you are a young person, you also need to face the fact that you will never grow old in this present system of things. ... All evidence in fulfillment of Bible prophecy indicates that this corrupt system is due to end in a few years. ... As a young person you will never fulfill any career that this system offers. If you are in high school and thinking about a college education, it means at least four, perhaps even six or eight more years to graduate into a specialized career. But where will this system of things be by that time? It will be well on the way toward its finish, if not actually gone!"

Watchtower, 10/15/69, pg. 622, pg. 623✍.... Seventh millennium from man's creation by Jehovah God would begin in less than ten years.

> **According to the Bible timetable, man's history on earth has been nearly 6,000 years. Adam was created in 4026 B.C.E., which means that six thousand years of human history end about the fall of 1975 C.E. We are in the great 7,000-year rest day of God, starting at the time He rested after the creation of Adam and Eve. There are, therefore, a thousand years left to run. Without Satan and his demons to disturb mankind it will indeed**

be a restful time. It will be like a Sabbath. Watchtower 7/15/67 pg. 446-7

The immediate future is certain to be filled with climactic events, for this old system is nearing its complete end. Within a few years at most the final parts of Bible prophecy relative to these "last days" will undergo fulfillment, resulting in the liberation of surviving mankind into Christ's glorious 1,000-year reign. What difficult days, but, at the same time, what grand days are just ahead! ❧Watchtower 5/1/68 pg. 272

'What about the year 1975? What is it going to mean, dear friends?' asked Brother Franz. 'Does it mean that Armageddon is going to be finished, with Satan bound, by 1975? It could! It could! All things are possible with God. Does it mean that Babylon the Great is going to go down by 1975? It could. Watchtower 10/15/66 pg. 631

Notice what is encouraged in the Kingdom Ministry a year prior to 1975 (monthly internal JW newsletter)

Reports are heard of brothers selling their homes and property and planning to finish out the rest of their days in this old system in the pioneer service. Certainly this is a fine way to spend the short time remaining before the wicked world's end. —1 John 2:17 ❧Kingdom Ministry May 1974 pg.3

So, the society *was* putting out that "1975" was the year that THIS SYSTEM OF THINGS WILL COME TO AN END, meaning the wicked was going to be destroyed. Discussions at Circuit and District Assemblies, and local Kingdom Halls were given. Conversations about 1975 were every day talk. My mother stated to me "if you want to see your father again" this is the only true religion that gives millions of people hope for everlasting life here on earth. The earth will not be destroyed and all the people that died will live again. Jehovah's Witnesses believe in the resurrection, millions would rise from the grave and live again on a paradise earth forever. My mother was telling me all of this right after my father died. I would constantly ask, "Mommy, you sure?" My father meant everything to me. To see him alive again was to me GREAT! I was only 7 years old and I started thinking that when someone dies it was only temporary; everyone that died will be coming home in 1975. If this were true, my father would be home a year later after he died because my mother had gotten baptized and dedicated her life to Jehovah just in time. I was saying to myself that maybe this Jehovah's Witness religion was the real thing. But then I had reservations. I thought to myself "why isn't everybody a Jehovah's Witnesses." How come the Kingdom Halls were not filled to capacity from this belief? How come people were not trying to knock down the door to get in? I would think anybody in his or her right mind would want to see their loved ones that died again. At the end of 1975, I remember asking my mother "Is my father coming back to life? What happened to the events that would bring daddy home?" I was very confused. My mother said nothing. I was listening to the TV and radio hoping to see or hear something. I was looking out the window to see if my father was going to be coming through the door. Its 31 years later in the year 2006 and nothing has happened. So what did the society say? What happened? Why did the prophecy fail in 1975? What was the explanation the society gave?

9

This is what was said after the prophecy of 1975 failed. Note what the Watchtower said of those who followed that encouragement. This is a quote from the Watchtower magazine:

> "It may be that some who have been serving God have planned their lives according to a mistaken view of just what was to happen on a certain date or in a certain year. They may have, for this reason, put off or neglected things that they otherwise would have cared for. But they have missed the point of the Bible's warnings concerning the end of this system of things, thinking that Bible chronology reveals the specific date." Watchtower 7/15/76 pg.440

> "Did Jesus mean that we should adjust our financial and secular affairs so that our resources would just carry us to a certain date that we might think marks the end? If our house is suffering serious deterioration, should we let it go, on the assumption that we would need it only a few months longer? Or, if someone in the family possibly needs special medical care, should we say, 'Well, we'll put it off because the time is so near for this system of things to go? This is not the kind of thinking that Jesus advised." Watchtower 7/15/76 pg. 440

> "But it is not advisable for us to set our sights on a certain date, neglecting everyday things we would ordinarily care for as Christians, such as things that we and our families really need. We may be forgetting that, when the "day" comes, it will not change the principle

that Christians must at all times take care of all their responsibilities. If anyone has been disappointed through not following this line of thought, he should now concentrate on adjusting his viewpoint, seeing that it was not the word of God that failed or deceived him and brought disappointment, but that his own understanding was based on wrong premises."
Watchtower 7/15/76 pg. 441

So the members in Jehovah's organization fed way too much into the "1975" of biblical events. *HIS OWN UNDERSTANDING WAS BASED ON WRONG PREMISES.* After doing some research on the history of the organization, this isn't the first time the society had put emphasis on dates and made predictions.

In 1920 Joseph Rutherford, the second President of the Watchtower Society wrote a book entitled "Millions now Living Will Never Die" and he believed Armageddon was to come in 1925. He went to great lengths to prove this in the book he wrote. Notice this quote from his book:

"Therefore we may confidently expect that 1925 will mark the return of Abraham, Isaac, Jacob and the faithful prophets of old...." ❷Millions now Living Will Never Die pg. 89, 90

It was taught that 1925 would mark the end of seventy jubilees of fifty years each since the Israelites had entered Canaan. (Lev. 25:1-12) A. D. Schroeder of the Governing Body states: "It was thought that then the remnant of Christ's anointed followers would go to heaven to be part of the Kingdom. And that the faithful men of old, such as Abraham, David and others, would be resurrected as princes to take over the government of the earth as part of God's kingdom." Now how was this information put forth to the witnesses who read this material? Was it said as a mere possibility or even a probability, or was it said with such authority that it was understood to be a certainty? Notice the following quotes:

> **"We have no doubt whatever in regard to the chronology relating to the dates of 1874, 1914, 1918, and 1925. It was on this line of reckoning that the dates 1874, 1914, and 1918 were located; and the Lord has placed the stamp of his seal upon 1914 and 1918 beyond any possibility of erasure. What further evidence do we need? Using this same measuring line.... it is an easy matter to locate 1925, probably in the fall, for the beginning of the antitypical jubilee. There can be no more questions about 1925 than there were about 1914. Watchtower May 15, 1922"**

There you have it. My mother never mentioned 1975 to me there after. She and everyone else in the organization acted like it never happened. Despite nothing happening in 1975, my mother continued on in the faith. The 1975 fiasco caused the organization to lose thousands of members. It didn't faze my mother at all. In fact, In the fall of 1975, my mother bought a brand new Cadillac Fleetwood automobile that she still has today in the garage; 69,000 original miles on it. She didn't have a driver's license nor could she drive but she buys a brand new car. I guess since Armageddon wasn't taken place, and my father wasn't coming home to see us, we might as well be chilling in a brand new car to ride to the Kingdom Hall. My sister was going to be driving; she was happy.

Wonder where the money came from? It wasn't from the society, I can tell you that! Buying that car drew the attention of 'worldly' and 'spiritual' alike. Let me explain something about my mother. My mother is in a different category when it comes to dealing with people. When my mother is questioned about her activities, she just answers people in an unconventional manner. The person interrogating my mother is sometimes left wondering if my mother gave them a direct answer. That person is never satisfied with the answer. Questioning my mother on anything that she feels isn't your business, you are asking to get told off in a polite and gentle way and any questions that were asked were completely ignored. I know it didn't suit many in the Kingdom Hall that questioned my mother on different things. But guess what? My mother couldn't care less. She wasn't about to change. After 1975, going in to the late 1976, my mother wasn't compromising to the organization's polices, at least not all of them. My mother followed only the policies that would benefit her, the policies that were convenient for her to follow and whatever non-spiritual activities she was doing. The organization was 5 steps behind her but right on her tail.

CHAPTER THREE: AFTER 1975

I was taken out of Public School 118 during my 2nd grade semester and put into a private school called the Queens School, located in Kew Gardens, Queens. My mother could see how my father's death affected me and wanted me isolated to a smaller classroom environment. The fact that Armageddon didn't come and my father wasn't coming home from the graveyard didn't help matters either. My mother started to have me see a psychologist around this time to make sure my head was emotionally straight and make sure my father's death or the so-called Armageddon fiasco wasn't going to affect my concentration in school. My mother also worried that my father told me something right before he died and I was keeping it a secret from her. I was getting bombarded with questions about any last conversations I had with him. My mother was so convinced that my father and I had a secret that she instructed the psychologist to have me discuss my last conversions with him over and over until something came out. When the psychologist probed me over and over about my father's whereabouts before he died, she suggested to my mother that this possible secret could be buried deep inside my subconscious memory and that she should look into getting me hypnotized. My mother HAD to find out this secret! An appointment was made for me to meet with a hypnotist. Days before my scheduled hypnosis was to begin, my mother cancelled the appointment and no longer was interested in having me hypnotized. Apparently, she had discussed the matter of having me hypnotized with the Elders of the congregation. She was instructed not to go forth with me being hypnotized. As it turns out, Jehovah Witnesses forbids Hypnosis. Their view on hypnosis is that it allows your mind to be opened and taken over by Satan the devil and his demons to control your thoughts. No objections were made from my mother and I continued to have

14

emotional issues. I was having nightmares and sleeping with the light on at night and crying a lot. By the first week in school I had already hit a kid with my Fat Albert lunch box because he was calling me names and said something about my father. It was going to be a long year. There were a lot of changes going to this school. This was my first time on a school bus, even though it was a yellow van. I also noticed the teachers and kids looking at me strangely when I did not salute the flag. Jehovah Witnesses believe that saluting the flag is a form of idol worship. My mother had already told school administration that we were Jehovah's Witnesses and we don't salute the flag. I was not to partake in the holiday activities or birthday celebrations, including my own. I couldn't even sing the national anthem. This is probably the reason I don't know the words to the national anthem or the Pledge of Allegiance to this day.

I went to the Queens School for almost 3 years until they closed their doors due to bankruptcy. My mother came across another private school that had an education curriculum that was based on the philosophy of a lady named Dr. Maria Montessori. Dr. Maria Montessori was an Italian physician; in fact she was the first female physician in Italy that became interested in education while caring for mentally challenged children. She worked in a psychiatric clinic in Rome in 1905. In 1907, Montessori continued shaping her learning model by opening "A Children's House" for pre-school children living in the slums of San Lorenzo. With her scientific background to guide her, she observed how young people learned best when engaged in purposeful activity rather than simply being fed information. She drew upon her clinical understanding of children's growth and development in constructing an educational framework that would respect individuality and fulfill the needs of the "whole child." Dr. Montessori's pioneering work created a blueprint for nurturing all children –learning disabled to gifted—to become the self-motivated, independent and life-long learners that are the ultimate goal of today's educational reform movement.

The closest Montessori school my mother found was on Yellowstone Blvd down the street from Queens Blvd in Forest Hills, Queens. I attended the school from 1977 to 1979. There were kids from all different walks of life. My friend Peter was from Zaire, Africa. There was a kid from Japan, and another named Sebastian who was from Scotland. Though my mother told school administrators that she was a Jehovah Witness, barring me from participating in holiday or birthday functions, I did anyway. I participated in some but not all. My participation was eating the cake and drinking soda. I didn't sing "Happy Birthday", but I ate lovely. The Montessori School didn't have any physical education classes or a gym. It did, however, offer physical education through tennis and swimming at the YMCA (Young Men's Christian Association). My mother thought it was a great idea even though Jehovah Witnesses are not supposed to be involved with any organization that's part of the world or any ties to Christianity. I asked her about taking karate lessons and she said, "No! Taking up karate was not allowed by Jehovah Witnesses." The Witnesses in our congregation didn't know what type of school I was attending, and my mother didn't mention it. I found it funny how I was able to attend the YMCA but not celebrate holidays and birthdays and salute the flag. Could it be that my mother didn't know Jehovah's Witnesses were not suppose to be involved with the YMCA? Maybe this was her way of not over doing it. Maybe in her eyes she really didn't join the YMCA directly? In any case, I was now 9 years old; my sister was 19 and had just graduated from high school the year before. She was now working. My sister began hanging with a wild bunch of people, though she still was going to the Hall with my mother and me. There were even 1 or 2 girlfriends that she would hang with that also went to the Kingdom Hall. My sister went out on a date with a teenager from the Kingdom Hall named Steve. They went to see the premier opening of the movie *Star*

Wars. Guess who had to tag along with them? You guessed it...ME! So I tagged along on my sister's date to see "Star Wars" at a movie theatre in Flushing, Queens. It was the best movie I ever saw at that time. My sister had to watch me more than ever now because my mother was always working and my sister hated it. Everywhere my sister was, I was right there with her. My sister and I would be at her friend's house playing music and dancing and talking about the clubs and smoking and drinking. She tried to get me to smoke a cigarette and I coughed for hours after that. It's probably the reason why I hate cigarettes to this day. My sister would have to wait until after 11:00 o'clock at night to get out of me having to tag along with her. She was solo with her girlfriends *and these weren't the young girls from the Kingdom Hall either.* However, when my sister was forced to 'baby-sit' me, she showed me a good time. She took me to my first park jam in South Side Jamaica, Queens. It was over at Lincoln Park in 1977. We went with her new 'worldly' boyfriend that she had just met at a CB club she belonged to. Her friend Judy was also there with a boyfriend. My sister and I came home around 1:00 AM and my mother was livid because I was only 9 or 10 and supposed to have been home. My sister was working and going to the Kingdom Hall with us (she had no choice either) but she was also partying, drinking, smoking, and having a ball. She was just doing what 19 year olds do, but my mother thought it was getting way out of control. One Sunday morning my sister came home from hanging out all Saturday night. The door was locked and she couldn't get in. She started ringing the doorbell and knocking on the door frantically. My mother ignored the incessant ringing and knocking at the door. My mother made my sister wait; she didn't open the door until she was good and ready. When my mother finally opened the door she ordered my sister to get herself together by drinking some coffee. She told her to wash up because she and I were going to the Sunday meeting at the Kingdom Hall. But oddly enough, at the last minute my mother decided not to go. So my sister and I took her car to attend the Sunday meeting without our mother. We arrived back at the

17

house around 12:30 PM and we notice my mother in her Cadillac with her girlfriend. My mother motioned for my sister and me to get into the Cadillac with them. We never went into the house and paid little attention to where my mother's girlfriend was driving us. We asked where we were going. My mother, never one to give a straight answer said, "To the Bronx." We got into Manhattan and drove towards the 42nd Street Bus terminal. Then I asked, "Why are we going to the bus terminal?" My mother stated, "We have to pick someone up." My mother got out and went into the bus terminal only to return to pop open the trunk of the car. She said for my sister to get out of the car and come with her. The next thing I saw was my sister on the bus looking at me crying. My mother came back to the car and we parked by the bus to make sure my sister didn't sneak off. The bus driver got on the bus after closing the luggage door and sat in the driver's seat. The entire scene was slow and dramatic, my sister crying. <u>EVERYTHING</u> that belonged to her was now on the bus. I waved at my sister and cried, wondering what was going on. The bus pulled off and I waved at her, both of us crying. I asked my mother, "What's going on with my sister? Where is she going?" My mother gave me a serious look and said, "I've just sent your sister to Virginia on the bus. If you get out of line, I'm sending you away on the plane!" I laugh about it now because sometimes I think to myself that might've been better. We got back home and I went into the attic where my sister stayed. There was nothing. Not even a sock. My mother had packed up everything my sister owned while we were at the Kingdom Hall earlier that day. Neither of us had a clue. My sister didn't have a chance to call her friends, job, or make arrangements for anything. Just like that she was gone.

I had no outlet now that my sister was gone. I had no one to talk to and no one to share my pain with who would understand what I was going through. I was alone. And as far as the Kingdom Hall was concerned, I was on my own. This was tough because now instead of my sister looking after me while my mother was at work or after school, I was going to be staying with some Jehovah's Witnesses after school and sometimes the weekend. My mother made sure I was going to be staying with someone she trusted but also someone that was spiritual and could handle me. I've stayed with numerous Jehovah's Witness families. Most of them didn't have kids my age to play with and were STRICT as hell. Over a 3-year span, I must have stayed with 12 Jehovah's Witnesses families and 5 Worldly families. All of them were nice but somewhere down the line they just couldn't handle me. My mother just didn't want to pay the money to have someone watch me and so the next best thing was to leave me in the car. There were many times I stayed in the car for 12 hours, either in the middle of summer or in the freezing winter. Several times I slept in the car because my mother's work hours were 7:00 at night to 7:00 in the morning. I would have to stay there the entire time. My mother would bring out a plate of food and some items to read and then go back inside. It all depended on what patient she had to work for. There was a patient my mother had that was located in Fresh Meadows, Queens. The patient was senile. My mother would bring me into the house to use the bathroom and hide me in another room to eat and watch some TV. Then it would be back to the car until she got off around 7:00 PM. This mostly would be in the summer months when I wasn't in school. There were times during the school year that my mother had to work nights for a patient in Forest Hills, Queens and I couldn't stay home. My mother would take me along with her to work. I had to stay in the car and do my homework. Extreme measures forced me to bring a radio, some pillows, and a comforter to sleep in the car all night. My mother would come out to check on me periodically. She would start up the car so I could have heat for about 30 minutes. She would bring me something to eat and back inside she went. She did this for a while because she couldn't find anyone to watch me. One place I LOVED staying at was in the Bronx with one of my mother's best friends named Sattie (who I call Aunt Sattie). She wasn't a witness but they were friends long before my mother became a Jehovah Witness. My mother didn't have to worry about being bombarded with questions from Sattie. My Aunt Sattie stayed over by the Allerton Ave train stop off the number 2 train and she lived around the corner across the street from the park on Britton Street. The area was very quiet and had an urban feel unlike Queens at that time. I saw Hip Hop flourish at the park across from Aunt Sattie. They would be jamming and playing records! I could go over and watch as long as my Aunt Sattie could keep her eye on me. No one rhymed but the DJ, who was Puerto Rican; He was cutting up this break beat on a record called "I can't stop". Other Puerto Ricans were break dancing and pop locking. It was amazing back then to see because coming from Queens this was something that was still an "uptown thing". The Bronx had this street culture on lock and at a level that didn't reach Queens until some years later. The day I saw "hip hop" at this Bronx Park, I started wondering if I could do something like this and be a Jehovah Witness and attend the Kingdom Hall. That was a day I'll never forget; it had a big impact on me later on. When I stayed in the Bronx with Aunt Sattie, I didn't go to the Kingdom Hall and would miss meetings and field service on the weekends. My mother didn't like that. She had to find someone closer to home to watch me, someone who went to the Kingdom Hall, and at the same time wasn't going to ask her a zillion questions. She wanted me around someone zealous in the truth that took no-nonsense and was 100% SPIRITUAL. It had to be someone my mother trusted greatly and didn't attend our kingdom hall. I just didn't think it was going to be a one of the most spiritual and zealous Jehovah Witness woman that was living. I was going to be long summer.

Chuck D from the rap group Public Enemy said in the beginning of a song *"1989!!! ANOTHER SUMMER! GET DOWN, SOUNDS OF THE FUNKY DRUMMER"* while it should've said, *"1979"!!! ANOTHER SUMMER! GET DOWN, PAIN FOR JEHOVAH'S BROTHER".* That's how I felt about field service for the summer of '79. My mother was working 12-24 hour shifts as a private home aid attendant for a state agency; she was making good money and I had to stay with a very zealous Jehovah's Witness lady by the name of Sister Mintz for the summer. My mother said she just couldn't find anyone else to look after me. I think she could have, but I also believe she wanted to help Sister Mintz out as well. The woman was a full time pioneer and also "one of the anointed." Jehovah Witnesses believe that there are two separate classes of people that will have eternal life. The organization teaches that the book of Revelation Chapter 7 verses 9-17 discusses one group of people will have "the earthy hope" called "the great crowd", in which that group will live here on a paradise Earth forever. The second class, which is talked about in the book of Revelation Chapter 14 verses 1-4 mentions another class of people that will be part of a "heavenly class or government" which consists of a number of "144,000". These individuals will reign in the heavens with Jesus Christ and Sister Mintz was part of this group. Being that she was a full time pioneer, it meant she devoted all her time in the preaching work, which was at least 90 hours a month, That included door-to-door preaching, street witnessing, bible studies, return visits, and informal witnessing. That meant for the next 2 to 3 months I would be putting in 90 hours or more along with her. My mother made sure to screw up my summer. Staying with Sister Mintz was no happy occasion, especially if you weren't the most spiritual child ... like me. When it came to someone faithful and loyal to Jehovah and that lived her life accordingly, Sister Mintz was that person. If my mother had any worries before about me not attending the meetings, those worries were now gone. Sister Mintz wasn't going to let that happen, and I had a lot of respect for her. I truly believe that whatever religion she worshipped, she was going to be blessed. She just happened to be a Jehovah's Witness. The first night I stayed with her she explained the rules. There was no late night television; and the television went off at 11:00 PM. I would get up at 5:00 AM during the week, shower and eat breakfast. I would have the reading of the daily text once up. There were no telephone calls unless it was to my mother. Other rules consisted of no cursing or swearing, going out for field service, going on bible studies with her, attending all of the meetings, no comic books, no *Twilight Zone*, no *Star Trek*, no *I dream of Jeannie*, no *Bewitched*, no rated R movies, no girls, no *Lucky Charms* cereal, no demonist or horror movies. It was going to be a long summer. A typical weekday started off like this: wake up at 5:00 in the morning, shower up and have breakfast, read the daily text from the yearbook, get ready for street-work at the Jamaica bus terminal or in front of May's department store on Jamaica Ave and 168th street. There were other pioneers joining us there so it wasn't like we were there alone. Sister Mintz and I would head over to the Jamaica bus terminal first. I would be in a suit and tie, my bible book-bag strapped to me. I would be holding up the latest issues of the Awake and Watchtower magazines. If someone were interested, I would approach them and say, "I have the latest issues of the *Watchtower* and *Awake* discussing God's Kingdom. If you are interested the magazines could be yours for 30 cents for the cost of print." I would be walking up and down chasing everyone that passed by on his or her way to work. This would be from 6:00 AM to 8:00 AM, right in the middle of rush hour at the bus terminal. I was glad no one passed me that I knew. However, I was only 12 years old. We would be at the bus terminal until 8:00 in the morning before heading over to May's department store. We would repeat the process of holding up the magazines in front of May's department store until 9:00. Then we would start heading back towards "the group" for door-to-door field service. We would first meet up as a group, usually at a publisher's home. There we would discuss the daily text and the "territory" we would be working. There would be a group of 12 to 20 publishers on a good day. Sister Mintz didn't drive so we would catch a ride into the "territory". The "territory" was usually street blocks made up into "territory squares". We would work it depending on how many publishers we had for the day. We had a list of addresses that we needed to do "return visits" which was grueling. These visits applied to publishers that received some interest at a home, whether it was from a discussion, interest of a bible study, or if someone in that home wanted us to come back. We also had a list of "not at homes" that recorded all the homes where we weren't getting an answer or a dog was there, and we didn't enter the premises. We also had a list of "homes with people with no interest" which meant they were rude or they caused many problems when trying to approach their door. There also was a list of homes that we knew of people that were disfellowshipped or "Apostates" who were expelled or went against the organization. We were instructed not to go to there home or door and not to have any contact with such individuals. It might be a little different now from what I was told because the organization wants the number of disfellowshipped ones to be reduced by getting them into bible studies and getting them reinstated. So if a disfellowshipped person comes to the door, the information would be noted and that information would be handed over to the Elders.

CHAPTER FOUR: FIELD SERVICE

I was in field service or door-to-door ministry at an early age. It started out only on the weekends, Saturday morning or Sunday afternoons. Going out in field service was something I had to get used to. Whether it was going door-to-door in the rain, cold, sleet, snow, in the hot blazing sun, being chased by dogs or having people scream at you to leave *"NOW"* or else they would sick their dog on you. Other times people would simply say "I'm not interested!" slamming the door in your face! Often I would knock or ring the bell and the person in the house would be looking right at me, but they would act like I was invisible. They knew it was Jehovah's Witnesses. All the jokes that were being said about Jehovah's Witnesses didn't start occurring until sometime in the late 1980's. We hear all kind of Jehovah's Witness's jokes now. Comics love to talk about Jehovah's witnesses knocking on someone's door or ringing their doorbell. I remember entering a yard and didn't notice or see a "beware of dog" sign. I was with another member and a dog came from out the backyard. There that dog was, right by the door, waiting for any movement. Some of the other members we were working with came by the fence and drew attention towards them. When the dog took his eyes off us for a second, myself and the other brother that was with me ran for the fence and jumped. We were pretty shaken up, but still alive. From that point on I made it a habit to leave the gate open so the dog could run out through it so we could avoid being bitten. I felt guilty sometimes ringing people's doorbell and waking them up, especially on Saturday or Sunday morning. Sometimes I would fake ringing the doorbell but I wasn't a big fan of it until I got older. Here is my reason why: My mother would buy the <u>Watchtower</u> and <u>Awake</u> magazines after the Thursday night theocratic ministry school was over. She would buy other literature for door-to-door ministry. So once she bought the literature and made a contribution to the contribution box, whatever money I received from placing the Watchtower and Awake magazines and books I kept. The more magazines and books I sold or placed, the more money I had for myself. I would come home sometimes with $5.00 to $15.00 and that would be enough to buy candy, potatoes chips, sodas and White Castle hamburgers. That was a lot of money back in the 1970's. Ringing someone's doorbell, and practicing what I was going to say to get some money, made my task much easier. I remember another time I was working the territory off Murdock Avenue and 202nd street. The weather was COLD with a capital 'C'. It was Sunday morning. The weather was around 20 degrees and it just started snowing. On my Mickey Mouse watch it read that it was only 9:45 AM. I was complaining on how cold I was. The brother that was taking the lead told me that we would be finished with the territory around 11:00 AM and then we'd do some return visits. The return visits weren't always in walking distance and needed a car to get to. Return visits would be spread out everywhere on our route and doing return visits allowed us to sit in the car; allowing us to be warm instead of being in the freezing cold. That hour and fifteen minutes walking door-to-door seemed like four hours. I complained that my feet and ears were frozen and that my fingers were numb. I complained damn near the whole time that I was freezing to death; but I was loyal to Jehovah. You would think that once the snow started coming down, we would change plans. We were preaching the good news of the Kingdom during a snowstorm. My hours of field service averaged 10 hours a month, which was around 3 hours a weekend. As summer months approached, with nicer weather, and school was let out, my mother wanted more hours from me in field service. I complained, but had to go out anyway. I would even put in fifteen or maybe twenty hours during the summer months, but my mother wanted me to go out in field service more often and work territory that was closer to our house.

Field service was something I was ok with at first because I was just 9 or 10 years old when I first started. Also, the area where I lived wasn't in our territory so I didn't have to worry about going door-to-door in my neighborhood, which was cool. The "Murdock Ave" congregation territory consisted of Hollis, a small part of St. Albans, Cambria Heights, and Queens Village, and a small part of Jamaica, Hollis Hills, and Elmont, Long Island. I was fond of Elmont because the further away I was from home, the better chance I had not seeing anyone I knew.

I was allowed to ring the doorbell when I did field service. I had my presentation down to perfection. It was simple and straight to the point. I would ring the bell twice and if you came to the door I would say, "Good Morning, my name is Daniel. This is my companion (brother or sister) and we were talking with your neighbors about enjoying life on this paradise earth forever. Is this a discussion you would be interested in? If not, would you like to have a copy of our latest issue of the *Watchtower*? You can read about how we are living in the last days of this wicked system and what you can do to live forever on this paradise earth. With its companion magazine, *The Awake*, the magazines are only 30 cents, for the cost of print. I said this presentation until I was grown. As time went on, congregations grew and so did the territory. Remember I mentioned earlier that our physical address wasn't in our territory? Well guess what? A third congregation was added to our Kingdom Hall called "Bellaire Park Congregation" and a re-zoning of territory was done. The block that we lived on was now part of the "Murdock Congregation." This meant whenever I was in field service, and the territory to be worked was to include my neighborhood, I suddenly came down with a cold and had to leave. I remember one Sunday afternoon, after the Watchtower meeting was over, my mother said "I HAD TO GO OUT IN FIELD SERVICE with the group!" I asked the ministerial servant who was taking the lead for Sunday's door-to-door activity where we were going to be and he stated, "We will be going door-to-

door over by Farmers Blvd and 112ᵗʰ and Murdock Avenue and 194ᵗʰ street."
He said, "That's your area, Danny." We should see you witnessing a lot this
afternoon." I laughed, "Yes, you should." But in the back of my mind I was
saying, "Not today." Everybody knew my mother and I went to the Kingdom
Hall but never saw me out on the block preaching. It wasn't going to happen
this Sunday either. I hurried up and left. I told my mother I had to go home
because I had to use the bathroom. I told her my stomach was hurting. My
mother came through the door two hours later and asking where I had been. I
told her plainly, "I'll do field service in any other neighborhood but I'm not doing
my area." I promised her next week I would go out with the group in Elmont;
she was fine with that. That lasted a few years until my mother got me back
real good. We had to work our neighborhood again but this time my mother
tricked me telling me to ride with another brother for return visits; he would
drop me off at home. I agreed, not knowing the brother only had 2 return
visits. While taking me home I saw a bunch of people from my congregation
on my block. The brother parked his car in front of my house and joined the
group. When I got out the car, the publishers from my congregation started
pairing me up to work with this older brother. The older brother said to me,
"Isn't this a blessing from Jehovah that we were just in time to work your
block." I rolled my eyes and said,"Yeah, isn't this coincidence?" I heard it that
day and all that week from everybody that saw me. I was asked questions on
purpose from my block friends just so they could laugh at me. It was brutal.
I remember another incident when I was in field service in Cambria Heights,
going door-to-door with the residing Elder. He was the head of all of the other
Elders in the congregation. I knocked on the door and lo'-and-behold, this girl
I'd been trying to get a date with lived at the house. She opened up the door
and saw me. She said while chuckling, "Hi, Danny!" I was so nervous that
the brother I was with just started talking. The brother asked, "So you know
Brother Danny?" She answered teasingly, "He goes to my school. Maybe we
can talk about the bible tomorrow at school." I was so embarrassed. She saw

me the next day in school and laughed her ass off. She was telling all her girlfriends I was a Jehovah's Witness and that I tried to sell her a Watchtower and Awake magazines. I guess you know I didn't want to see her anymore. I ducked her every chance I could. From that point on I started faking ringing the doorbell. I heard about people doing this (including my sister). I was getting older and popular. The last thing I needed was someone from school or the neighborhood to see me going door to door. The last time I remember going into field service was in the fall of 1987. I'm sure it hasn't changed much since then. I do know that when Jehovah's Witnesses approached me at my cousin's house in '91, they came to the door and I said, "Good Morning!" They would say their presentation and I politely listened, already knowing how it went. In the middle of the presentation I came out abruptly, confessing, "I'm disfellowshipped!" They would *"ooooh"* and *"ummmm"* and, *"Okay. Have a good day."* Then they would take off running like they just saw a character from *The Munsters*.

CHAPTER FIVE: CIRCUIT AND DISTRICT ASSEMBLIES

My mother started going to the Circuit and District Conventions in 1974, before she got baptized with her girlfriend that lived around the corner. My mother's friend told me my father used to drop her and my mother off at Aqueduct Race track in Ozone Park, Queens, for the District Conventions. The District Conventions or District Assemblies are bigger than the circuit assemblies. Certain districts consisted of as many as 100 congregations, and no less than 20 congregations attend the District Assemblies. The Circuit Assemblies would consist of no more than 20 congregations and no less than 5. There is a circuit overseer that visits the congregations twice a year and a district overseer that visits the congregation once a year. The District overseer presides over the entire district of congregations, while the circuit overseer presides over the circuit of congregations. When I started going to the Kingdom Hall, our circuit assemblies were in Washington Heights, Manhattan at an old church. Over the years the location changed to an old movie theatre on Green point Avenue and 47th street in Long Island City, Queens. It was big enough to hold the several congregations that attended while maintaining the noise level to a minimum. The area was perfect for lunch when there was an intermission. Restaurants like White Castle, Wendy's, McDonalds, Burger King, Pizza shops and Spanish diners would be in walking distance. The Organization tried to encourage members to eat inside during intermission and not patronize out to the "worldly" establishments. The Organization provided food like burritos, chili, hamburgers, ice cream, floats and sodas. I started working at the circuit assembly just to get free food. I eventually stopped because I wanted to go outside with my friends to eat and after awhile, the food wasn't that great anyway. The Organization no longer provides food at the assemblies. They want to provide more spiritual food than physical food. The society started encouraging "the friends" to bring their own food.

People that wanted to dedicate their lives to Jehovah and show their dedication publicly were baptized at the Circuit or the District Assemblies. The Circuit Assembly was usually held twice a year while the District Assembly was held only once a year. When we had our Circuit Assembly it was on Saturday and Sunday; we wouldn't have a Thursday night meeting. The Circuit Assembly usually started around 9:40AM, breaking for lunch around 11:35 and returning around 1:00PM. A series of discussions or talks by Congregation Elders, Circuit and District overseers, members of Bethel and sometimes a member of the governing body could be heard blaring from the speakers. We would be writing and taking notes, clapping when any good kingdom news was mentioned in regards to membership growth, preaching work growth, publisher growth, Kingdom Halls being built, the growth at the *Watchtower Farm* and new publications. There were thousands that met at the circuit and district assemblies to fellowship with one another. We would discuss how the "faithful and discreet slave" provided the spiritual food we were receiving to us. We would talk about how this food was available through God's will, and how we had been blessed with the food we were receiving. Of course gossip was always discussed among the friends about who was with whom, what sister and brother had hooked up, and whom we saw at the assembly that was recently disfellowshipped or shunned from the organization. We would gossip about who was at the assembly just to meet a mate and return back into the truth.

I met several of my Jehovah's Witness girlfriends at the district and circuit assemblies from all over Queens and Long Island. I met two in particular that stood out and thought they were pretty cool. One was from Far Rockaway and another was from Elmont. The girl from Elmont, Long Island, I met her at the District Convention at Belmont Park and we kicked it for a while over the phone because her parents had her on lockdown and wouldn't allow her to have much freedom. She wasn't a worldly type of girl, but she was curious about sex. When I finally did see her, it was around my birthday. It was hot, and she was home alone during the day. She saw me at the door and we wasted no time. I came in the house and we began kissing. Our clothes came off! But she took me by surprise when she said, "Do me from behind. It's that time of the month," So, I obliged, but I was nervous. This was our first time and my first anal sex ever. We had been talking for months over the phone long enough to feel comfortable with each other. We knew we wouldn't rat on each other and that our parents wouldn't find out. I had heard she took the spiritual route and I think she had gotten married to a brother "in the truth" and baptized some years later. If they both "in the truth", meaning they are dedicated and baptized witnesses, anal and oral sex is forbidden and out of the question even if you are married. The organization teaches that these sex acts are a form of uncleanness and can be reasons of being disfellowshipped. I wonder would the wife or the husband tell the Elders what they're doing. I seriously doubt it unless she or he told someone else "in the truth" about his or her sex life and they are reported to the elders.

The second girl I met that was from Far Rockaway, Queens. I met her at the circuit assembly at Green Point Ave in Long Island City, Queens. She was an average looking girl, but I thought she was pretty because of the way she made herself up. Her clothes made her look better than she really was. But then again I couldn't be picky. I needed to get as many numbers as I could get, just in case some of the numbers I were getting from girls were fake numbers. I needed backups. It didn't matter how far from me they lived. I didn't mind traveling somewhere. My running partner and friend Tim told me the girl wasn't all that, but I got her number anyway. I went out to Far Rockaway to see her and my man Tim was right, she wasn't attractive at all. We were around her neighborhood, and after awhile of walking through her block, I started to notice we were getting stares from a lot of people. It appeared that this chick wasn't liked at all. Some words came from a group of girls and the next thing I know; some guys were getting into to jump me. The young woman did nothing. It was time to make a b-line to the Mott Avenue train station where I could catch the A train instead of waiting for a bus. I realized the train stop was four blocks from where I was. Even in the distance I could see the train at the station preparing to leave. I just looked at this young woman, said nothing, and made like I was going into a corner store. I then took off running. It must have been six guys chasing me but I was always fast; I wasn't about to be jumped. They stopped chasing me when I got to the subway station. I hopped aboard and left her area for home. I called my man Tim and he cracked up laughing. "I told you that chick wasn't all that." That's what I get for thinking that just because she was down with Jehovah she would be cool. Everyone that was at the assembly with a suit on wasn't necessarily a good brother. Some were straight up hoodlums in suits. I came across some guys that from Brooklyn who were pretty wild for brothers that attended the kingdom hall. They didn't pull out guns or knives but were just straight up street. They were stealing burritos and sodas from food-stands. You would have thought they were "kingdom hall gangsters", like guys on the street corner when ready for a fight. I ran into them a couple of times at different assemblies. I just let them know that they wouldn't be the only ones that could get stupid at a district convention. It didn't matter if we were at the assembly and dressed up; my peeps and I were no spiritual saints either.

One year, at a District Convention held at Yankee Stadium, I had gotten into it with some guy. There were no other brothers around except us. We started to curse and get loud. We couldn't throw our hands up and fight because of where we were, but I told the guy to meet me outside. I rounded up some of my peoples including the Wild Brooklyn Brothers and I told them what had happened. They came with me outside of the stadium. We found the guy I had words with and we approached him and his peoples. It looked like a scene off a street corner. We started arguing about what was said earlier. To my surprise, the wild Brooklyn Brother's knew one of this guy's people. The brothers from Brooklyn told this guy that they don't want any beef and to squash it. We had about 15 guys to their 10 guys. Even though we weren't going to fight, it still showed the more numbers and strength. After arguing for 10 or 15 minutes, the other group walked off. None of us were going to fight at the District Assembly; someone just wanted to show who was the most street out of the group.

The Circuit assemblies had around 2,500 people in attendance. You couldn't hang out much like the District Assemblies. Working at the Circuit Assemblies, I was okay with. You pretty much were in a seat if there weren't any activities. There wasn't too much movement. Ministerial servants were everywhere because the area we were confined to was so small. Circuit Assemblies were a good place to see your homeboys. We could hang out and talk about when and where our district assemblies would be or, what gear we would be wearing. We would do our best to add a little urban flavor to what we were wearing. People's clothes were a good clue as to whether they were too spiritual or too worldly. For example, if you were wearing a pair of Playboys, Clarks, British Walkers, or Bally's shoes you probably was not the most spiritual publisher in the organization. If you were rockin' leather ties, sheepskins, leather bombers, leather fronts, sharkskins, and you weren't baptized yet, you probably weren't going to be baptized any time soon. A person's clothes also gave away where they were from. I could tell if someone was from Brooklyn, Long Island, or uptown just by his or her gear. In the following years, the Circuit Assemblies moved from the Green Point movie theater to another movie theater that was out in Flatbush, Brooklyn.

After a while the Circuit Assemblies moved to another movie theatre in Jersey City, New Jersey. The one in Jersey City was where I was baptized.

The District Assemblies were once a year in the summer. They were held from Thursday morning to Sunday afternoon. While the Circuit assembly was two days the District Assembly was four. This gave me greater time to get more phone numbers from girls. The organization would have District assemblies at various locations. Out of the 16 years or more that I was attending, the District Assemblies would be at held at various places like Yankee Stadium, Giants Stadium, Nassau Coliseum, and Belmont Park Racetrack. Of all the district assemblies I attended, the best ones were at Belmont Park. Belmont Park is a racetrack in Elmont, Long Island, right across the New York City border. It was only a 20-minute drive from the house. There were no restaurants around, and the organization served food and drinks. It was so comfortable and spacious. There would be thousands of witnesses and hundreds of women. This was the big convention. The organization would present "new light" on matters, new publications, and "talks" on several subjects. There were even reenactments of Bible stories and parables. They were beneficial in helping to see how things were done back in Biblical days. The District Assembly would have every congregation in the tri-state area. This was all the congregations in Brooklyn, Queens, The Bronx, Staten Island, Long Island, Manhattan, and some congregations from New Jersey and Connecticut. All this added up to more girls for me to choose from. My mother and I would find seats that were close to the stage, under the roof in case it rained. We would have sandwiches and drinks, and a pair of binoculars to see right on the stage. Belmont Park was very easy to get around and almost felt like a neighborhood event because we were so close to home. The very first time I went to the District Assembly I couldn't believe the organization was as big as it was. There were thousands of Jehovah's Witnesses worshipping at one gathering. I was also amazed about all the kids I could meet and eventually hang out with. Here was a place I could meet some Jehovah's Witnesses kids from other congregations whether they lived in Brooklyn or Queens or Long Island. If they appeared spiritual, my mother was cool with it because we all were down with Jehovah. It wasn't like I was associating with a Muslim or a Baptist or a Seven-Day Adventist. After all I was with Jehovah's people. For the first several years, I would sit with my mother during the "bible talks" and go to the bathroom just to hang out for thirty minutes and then return back to my seat. I would do this during the morning "talks". I would then hang out during the intermission, and again for 30 to 45 minutes during the afternoon "bible talks". My mother wasn't having me run around chasing girls and hanging out during the "talks" like I saw others doing. I wondered for a long time how will I be able to get out of my seat and hang out too. One year at the district assembly, I was hanging with my friend Kendu, who lived in my neighborhood, but attended another congregation. I was helping him distribute burritos to the food stands during the intermission when I saw my mother. She asked what I was doing. I said, "Some of the brothers need help taking fresh food to the stands. I was helping where the need was great." She saw whom I was with and knew him. Kendu said, "Hi, Sister C!" And my mother retorted, "Hi, sweetie. Are you helping the brothers as well?" He said, "Yes. Can Daniel continue helping me?" My mother said it was okay but that I needed to be back in my seat as soon as the intermission ended, my mother was fine with that. I told her excitedly I would and then took off running. I returned several minutes after the intermission and that was fine with my mother. I asked her if I could assist the brothers again because they really needed the help but she started getting skeptical. I assured her that Brother Nat from our congregation was one of the ministerial servants taking the lead in distributing all the food through out the convention. He would make sure I was working. I also assured my mother that I would be paying attention close to the talks. She spoke with Brother Nat to validate that he was indeed in charge of the food distribution and he really needed

35

help. He said yes. Afterwards, it was fine to work. He would make sure that I would be sitting somewhere listening to the talk and not running around goofing off. I received her approval with high honors. I started early the next morning. I volunteered with other young brothers from my Kingdom Hall, and some who were from other Kingdom Halls. We would take the burritos and sodas to all the food stands and come back to base and hang out. We weren't paying attention the "talks" blaring on the loudspeaker. We would be cracking jokes and playing the POOF game. Now to play the POOF game, we would open the powered coffee creamers and blow it in someone's face and go POOF! We'd laugh while powered coffee cream was all over a fellow brother's face and shirt. We ate and drank for free, having a great time not sitting in our seats. While we were working, we would be getting all kinds of phone numbers and meeting all kinds of girls from different congregations. I would see people I would only see at the Circuit and District Assemblies. I was meeting quite a few girls who were pretty and just as wild as me. One girl I met was from Staten Island. I could tell she wasn't anything spiritual. She had nothing that read spiritual written on her. I went to go see and hang out with her and her brothers and she drank more beer and smoked more weed than me. Everyone in the hood knew about her and her brothers. Unfortunately, nothing sexual happened between her and me. I would go visit her every weekend. This went on for a couple of months, but she lived too far. It took almost 2 hours to get to Staten Island from Queens on the bus and train. We kissed a couple of times, but that was it. I met some other girls from Flatbush, Brooklyn and they were pretty cool as well. I would go out to see them for a couple of years but nothing sexual would happen. We would talk about the bible, the organization, and what direction we wanted to go in life. Everybody said being a Jehovah's Witness was something we didn't see in our future. Some years later I bumped into one of those girls at a club. She obviously wasn't down with Jehovah. We hung out all night with our friends, driving around all night in Queens and Manhattan. We didn't get home until

8:00 AM the next morning. I later found out she was a distant cousin to my sisters and my brother from my mother's first marriage. I was the only child from my mother's second marriage.

At one District Assembly held at Belmont Park racetrack, I met a very pretty girl who was visiting from England. I was attracted to her immediately. She was a year or two older than me. All I remember about her was her accent ... and her body. She had that British accent that I so loved to hear. I met her while I was making deliveries to the food stands. We exchanged numbers and I called her that night. I couldn't talk long so we agreed to meet at a certain location the next day at the assembly. We continued seeing each other till the last day of the assembly, which was Sunday. When that Sunday arrived we started to kiss, feeling each other. I wasn't going to see her anymore because she was just here visiting family and going back to England. While working at the District Assemblies at Belmont Park, I found out that certain brothers would take girls to secluded areas to be alone with them. It would be in areas only workers and security had access to. I took this young woman to an area that was very secluded and air-conditioned. We started kissing and rubbing each other's body parts and it started to get very hot. Her bra came off and I could see her panties were soaking wet. I started kissing her legs and thighs, slowly making my way closer to her panties. I pulled them off and started having her as a tasty meal. This was my first oral sex encounter, and I enjoyed it. I had her body scent all over my face and had to remember to wash my face when I was done. She was begging me to stop but at the same time she wouldn't let go off my head and wouldn't let me come up for air. This continued on for 25 to 30 minutes. We continued right into the last prayer for the assembly. We finally stopped, getting ourselves together. We kissed one last time. It felt like time had stopped. It took another 5 minutes just to say," goodbye" and that was the last time I saw her. I thought, *"what if we had gotten together and even had gotten baptized together".* I would have lived a double life and fronted for Jehovah just to be with her. After she left, I went back to my workstation and told my boys what happened. I wasn't trying to brag, but it was something crazy to talk about because of where it happened. My friends looked at me like I was crazy; they were in total disbelief. Maybe they thought I went a little overboard.

CHAPTER SIX: TUESDAY NIGHT AND THURSDAY NIGHT MEETINGS

A lot of people always want to know what goes on behind close doors. They want to know what is discussed during the meetings at the Kingdom Halls and at the Tuesday night book studies conducted at a Witness home. So here is some insight on what's discussed at the meetings on Tuesday and Thursday nights. We used to have our Tuesday night book study at Sister Patti's home in her living room. This was the same Sister Patti's who aided my mother in the truth. Our Tuesday night book study would start around 7:00 PM, continuing for an hour. We would study one of the books the organization published, a specifically assigned published book. It was a small group of 12 to 20 people and we would start off the study with prayer. Only someone who was a baptized ministerial servant brother or an Elder could lead the prayer. After the prayer, the book study would review the reading from the week before. Then everyone would take turns reading, rotating from person-to-person. We would have about 15 pages to ready and study. The book would be chaptered with numbered paragraphs. If you were present you were reading. No matter if you had speech impediment, you were reading. Our congregation had two brothers that stuttered; one of those brothers belonged to our book study group. It took forever for him to read a complete sentence. It seemed like we would be there at the book study all night. Now, I was becoming a great reader. I took the opportunity to read more than the norm. No one had an issue with it because I was reading clear, with excitement, and a steady pace. I was coherent. As 8 o'clock approached, the book study would come to a close. We would be joined again in prayer. Afterwards, we would have refreshments and snacks while associating among ourselves for

15 to 20 minutes. As the night wore on, everyone would start heading towards his or her car or start walking home.

The Thursday night meeting started around 7:30. It would begin with the singing of a song from a book of songs published by the organization. From the song we would have opening prayer, and then, the opening of the meeting. This consisted of the first of two parts that made up the Thursday night meeting. There was a series of four Bible talks for the evening. The first Bible talk would start off the first part of the meeting. It would always be by a baptized brother who would talk about a certain subject that was already outlined by the organization. The first talk would last around 15 minutes. At 8 o'clock the congregation would split into two bible schools. Bible school one would remain in the main meeting area while Bible schools two would be in another room of the Kingdom Hall. The start of Bible talks 2 – 4 would begin in both schools. Each bible talk would last 5 minutes. There was always someone keeping time with a stop clock or watch. If a group went over 5 minutes, there would be a pencil or pen tapping against something indicating time is up. A male, usually someone that had just joined the Theocratic Ministry School, would always conduct Bible talk number two. A male that was new in the truth, or a male child or teenager sometimes gave it. A woman would conduct Bible talk number three, whether they were baptized or not. The same 5-minute limit would still apply. A brother that was baptized and experienced with giving talks would do Bible talk number four. If you were assigned bible talk number four, it would be safe to assume you wouldn't be assigned bible talk number two anymore. After the bible talks were done, there would be an intermission. We would stand up, start singing another song from the songbook, then stretch our legs and go to the bathroom or get some water. The people that went into bible talk two would return back to the main meeting area to rejoin everyone else. The singing of the song would be over and we would sit down for the second half of the meeting. The start of the second half would be general announcements for any upcoming events or weekly or monthly expense reports. Weekly or monthly kingdom funds were also discussed. We would discuss anything related to our building, or any new projects regarding our building. Another brother would come up to discuss other business related information in detail regarding something with our congregation. Residing Elders addressed more important announcements. These announcements were usually a death in the family, or encouraging visits to someone that was sick or in the hospital. The announcement could also mean that someone was about to be called out publicly and be disfellowshipped. Everyone would be very attentive looking around to see whose name would be called (and for what). The Elder would look straight into the audience and say Sister or Brother X has been disfellowshipped from the Christian Congregation and we are to no longer to associate with this individual. If the individual were there in attendance, no one would look at him or her and make them feel shameful. It would be a period of silence.

On the 2nd part of the Thursday night meeting, there were always bible talks given by the brothers on how to approach an unbeliever. There would be some examples on how to approach someone that isn't interested. Someone in the audience would play the part of the unbeliever while another person would act as a Jehovah's Witness. The person acting as a Jehovah Witness would pretend that he or she is knocking on the door of this unbeliever then start their sermon. The organization would create different scenarios on how to answer individuals we came across in field service. If the individual wasn't open minded for a discussion, the organization taught us not to become debatable and carry on to another home. If the individual showed a little interest, we were taught to place the latest issues of the *Watchtower* and *Awake* magazines. If further interest were there, maybe one of the society's publications, most likely, "the truth book" would be placed with them as well.

41

We were taught to get the individual's name and number, write down his or her address, and schedule a return visit. Hopefully a bible study would occur. The congregation would discuss how this demonstration went and if anything could've been different in the approach. Different feedback would be discussed among the publishers in the congregation. Their comments would be compared to what was outlined in the Theocratic Ministry school weekly pamphlet. The meeting would end with a song and prayer. After the meeting, my mother would tell me to get in line to retrieve the latest issues of the *Watchtower* and *Awake* magazines, or any other publications that were needed. If publications weren't available, I still needed to stay in line so my mother could put in an order. My mother would finally take my place after talking to some of her friends. Once she took my place in line, I would head outside and associate with both my kingdom halls cats and my worldly cats that were standing across the street. I would start to rhyme while hanging with the crew. I would rhyme about the Kingdom Hall and about Jehovah. Some of my Kingdom Hall friends would be on the look out to make sure no brothers were around. I would stay on the corner with them for about ten minutes hip-hoppin' and rhyming'. I would leave, giving them all a pound, telling them I'd see them at the next 'jam'. My mother would offer some members of the congregation a ride home if they lived close or missed their ride.

I joined the Theocratic Ministry School in my late teens, after years of ducking out and hiding. I was considered a late bloomer since the average age a child joins is 7 years old. I got away from not joining for many years until my mother wasn't taking no for an answer. My mother had put a whisper into Elder Brother Tyrone's ear that encouraged me to join. He stated, "It isn't that hard to do. You just have to read several scriptures from the bible and explain in detail what you read in five minutes." I replied, "That shouldn't be that hard". My mother thought I was going to get more spiritual, but that wasn't the case. I joined the Theocratic Ministry School after my mother started playing these mind games with me. She would say,"Look at little Chris, he is only 6 years old and he is reading the bible like a high scholar, I know you can do better than him." She tricked me into thinking I couldn't read well. I joined and was immediately assigned my first talk. I had to prepare what I was going to read, and I had to understand what I was reading. So a week before my first talk, I suddenly had to work overtime and canceled for a later date. A week before my first talk my mother bought me this fly wool suit from a men's clothing store in Green Acres Mall in Valley Stream, Long Island. She didn't have to buy a suit for me because I was working, but buying the suit was her way showing me where the power of control lay (and maybe a little form of encouragement). I was studying the bible verses over and over. I had to read and explain the verses in my own words. I was pumped up, ready, and determined not to back out again. That Thursday I came home from work and quickly threw on my new wool suit with matching shoes, ready for the stage. Thursday Theocratic Ministry School was started. I was scheduled to give talk number two. I heard my name called and stepped to the stage. I looked out into the audience and felt like there were a thousand people in attendance. But there were only 150 people, multiplied by my own imagination and anxiety. I opened up with a question first and then proceeded to the appropriate Bible book, chapter and verse. I would read my assigned verses and then explain their significance and meaning. I would continue reading to the end and explain again what I just read and then sum it all up in 5 minutes. I knew if I went passed the 5 minute mark there would be the loud tapping noise from the brother indicating the 5 minutes were up; the next sentence or comment had to be the last. But I made good time, right on the money. I finished right before the brother started tapping, and I received a loud applause. The applause was expected though. The congregation applauded after anyone finished their first reading. My mother proudly kissed me. You would have thought I just graduated college the way my mother was acting. She was praising me like I was the next circuit overseer to take the lead. Brother Tyrone came over and said I did an excellent job. He gave some pointers for my next talk that would be coming around three months. I didn't think three months was enough time, but it wasn't like this was hard either. I agreed and thanked him for the advice and encouragement. He let me see my publisher's report card, grading me on what I did well at and where I needed to improve. He stated I was a good speaker and had captured the audience's attention. However, I needed to look up a little more and catch my breath when speaking. Overall, I did well. I gave several more talks, but I was able to get out of doing a lot more because of my job. When I changed jobs and as I got older, the bible talks didn't disappear as I thought they would. Instead they increased; I had a total of four talks a year for two years straight. I never did a bible talk number four, which consisted of an advanced level bible talk with a more profound explanation of a particular bible topic. You had to be a baptized brother to do talk number-4. The Theocratic Ministry School is like a mini-Bible-school to prepare you for the ministry to be an effective and convincing speaker out in field service. You were taught how to defend the views of Jehovah's Witnesses without provoking a fight. You learned scriptures to reference. All the scenarios that could come up, we would discuss and act them out. The reason Jehovah's Witnesses prepare so much for bible studying and field service is because there is a lot of opposition in the world about what Jehovah's Witnesses do and preach. The more publishers they can train for the ministry, the more efficient the organization could run and be controlled. The Theocratic Ministry helped me get ready to do public speaking, not be shy and stand in front of an audience. It also taught me to read better and be articulate. I was also getting better at memorizing instead of reading from my note cards. My mother thought it would make me more spiritual. But, just because I was getting to know all the scriptures by heart, learning where all the bible books were, and how to get to a scripture the fastest, it meant nothing. I wasn't living it, and I didn't want to. I was getting ready for public speaking all right, but not to be an Elder or a ministerial servant in the Kingdom hall; it was to be an emcee on the microphone. It was ON!

CHAPTER SEVEN: THE HIP HOP JEHOVAH WITNESS

I heard a record on the radio late 1979 by the Sugar Hill Gang called "Rappers Delight". There was also another rap song called "King Tim III" by the R & B group named The Fatback Gang. It didn't really get much airplay and was hardly heard by mainstream and didn't blow up and go commercial like "Rappers Delight". I heard phrases like *"hip-hop and you don't stop"* and *"to the beat y'all"*. I was 12 years old and it seemed like I was young forever! I remember when I stayed in the Bronx with my Aunt Sattie in the late 70's that there was a park across the street from her apartment building on Britton Street. These young black and Puerto Rican teenagers were playing music, rapping and back-spinning records. I had no clue this was the real authentic Hip Hop and what I was hearing on the radio by the Sugar Hill Gang was just a watered down version of what I heard in the Bronx. We all know Hip Hop originated from the Bronx so there's no debating that. Hip-hop in Queens was a little different. Hip hop in Queens in 1979 and the early 80's were cats doing shout outs over R&B records and doing a DJ Hollywood from Harlem type of emceeing. Records like *"Good Times"* and *"Love is the Message"* and *"Listen to the Bass Play"* were the norm. No one really stood out at that time until RUN-DMC came in 1983. The emcees and rap groups in Queens were respectfully: The Disco Twins, Rat and Monkey, DJ Divine and Infinity Machine, The Clientele Brothers with MC Mikey D, Davey D, Black Rock and Ron, DJ Quick Silver, Super Lover Mc's, Herbie Luv Bug, Playboy Prince Charm and Romeo the American Gigolo, Spyder D, The Albino Twins, Eddie Cheba and The Cheba Crew, Allah Sounds, Grandmaster Vic and his crew from South Jamaica and Future Sounds (who were from around my way via Farmers Blvd) and dozen of others. They were all doing their thing respectfully, however the Bronx and Manhattan had Hip Hop on lock. I was seeing flyers and hearing hip hop tapes by the ones that were doing it back then and it was unbelievable. Groups like The Cold Crush Four, The Funky Four plus One, Fantastic Five, The Furious Five, DJ Grandmaster Flash, DJ Grand Wizard Theodore, Curtis Blow, Cosmic Force, Soul Sonic Force, Africa Bambattaa and his Almighty Zulu Nation, The Fearless Four, The Treacherous Three, Busy Bee, DJ AJ, Melle Mel, Kool Moe Dee, The L Brothers, DJ Doctor Rock from the Force emcees from Staten Island, DJ Kool Herc and The Herculoids, Lisa Lee, Sha Rock, Grandmaster Caz, Debbie Dee, Jazzy Five, DJ Whiz Kid, DJ June Bug, Crash Crew, Salt and Pepper emcees. They were performing everywhere like clubs, high schools, playgrounds, roller skating rinks, park jams, boat rides up the Hudson River, Community centers in the projects; they were everywhere and anywhere. I started collecting tapes from people outside of Queens, emulating these guys by saying their routines. I started imagined myself rockin' with them and pretending to be there at the party. I started saying some rhymes like the emcees I heard. Sometimes I added Jehovah's name or references to the Kingdom Hall in my rhymes. I didn't know about anything else, and it was the thing to be different and not say the same words, rhymes, and metaphors as others. You had to make up rhymes using different words, or with words that weren't being used. My early rhymes were about rockin' the house, rockin' girls, rockin' me here and there, and even the Kingdom Hall. This was around 1983. You also had to have a nickname. At the time I was calling myself "Disco Dan". My friend, who was nicknamed 'June', looked at me and said, "You look like a *geech*," and started laughing. I remember saying to myself *what the hell is a geech*? After that incident, I was watching one of my favorite movies called *Uptown Saturday Night* with Bill Cosby, Sidney Pointer, and Harry Belafonte. Harry Belafonte played this character named "Geechie Dan". That name was perfect since my real name was Daniel. I went by that name from that day on … even to the present. People heard of me all over NYC just from the name. So I started saying rhymes about my "Geechie Dan" persona; I became popular. I also rhymed at the Kingdom Hall and the Circuit and District Assemblies on the down low for some attention. I was meeting other teenagers that attended Kingdom Halls all over NYC that were into hip-hop. It seemed like we all had something in common because of the Kingdom Hall, saying rhymes with references to the Bible or the Kingdom Hall. It made me feel like I could "be down" with Jehovah and hip-hop. *Open up your Bible and lets start to reading, Adam and Eve lived in the Garden of Eden.* That was my first Bible rhyme. As time went on there would be more rhymes in reference to the bible or Jehovah like, "I got this girl bent over, all in the sofa, all in the name of Jehovah!" My friends thought I was crazy to be saying rhymes in reference to Jehovah in that manner. I called it being different.

In 1983 a record called "Sucker MC's and "It's like that" on the A-side came out by a group called RUN-DMC. They were from Hollis, Queens. In fact, they grew up and lived right down the street from the Kingdom Hall I went to on Hollis Ave and 201st. RUN-DMC took the hip-hop from the Bronx and Manhattan, added it with some Queens's flavor, and made it commercial. RUN-DMC is like the Queens' version of the Hip Hop group, *The Cold Crush 4.* The second stage of hip-hop has never been the same. You could actually make money and have a career doing hip-hop; it was no longer considered a fad. My mom was hearing me listening to rap music, rapping to myself downstairs in the basement. I told her that a group of guys in the neighborhood made a rap record. I told her they lived right down the street from the Kingdom Hall and they were called RUN-DMC; we all went to the same neighborhood schools. They weren't gangsters or drug dealers; they came from the same middle class upbringing as me. So, to me there was hope that going to the Kingdom Hall and rhyming co-existed. I saw where I could do hip-hop and still attend the Kingdom Hall. I figured out then that there were Jehovah Witnesses all over the tri-state area. The kids of these Jehovah

Witnesses were growing up "in the truth" unhappy, rebellious, and un-hip. Maybe hip-hop could be a way of unifying kids and showing peace and love all over the tri-state area. I heard stories that there were a few Jehovah Witnesses in the music business. Michael Jackson and his family were Witnesses. I heard George Benson was one. They were all successful, especially Michael Jackson. I thought that if Jehovah could bless Michael Jackson then He could bless me in hip-hop. My mom would laugh and say, *"Hip hop is a fad"* and *"It's cute but no career type of thing"*. My mom constantly came to the basement at night to turn the music down because I was listening to the radio late at night. She could feel the bass of the music all the way to her bedroom and she would get pissed off because she would be on the phone trying to talk. She would tell me to go to bed around 10:30 or 11:00 PM, but the radio station wasn't playing hip-hop until 1:00 AM. I had to get up for school in the morning. The radio station was WHBI 105.9 FM, the first to play hip-hop music. The DJ for the late night rap show was named "Mr. Magic". He would play all the new rap songs and demos. He got to be so popular that he received his own show on commercial radio, which was on WBLS 107.5 years later. After he went off the air around 3:00 AM, there was another two-hour show called *"The World Famous Supreme Team Show"*. They used to play the entire record of a break beat, which was unheard of then, and provide the name. They even had live emceeing and DJs from the tri-state area of NYC doing guest appearances. You could call up the radio station and send out live dedications to your girl, girlfriends, and your homeboys. Your name would be said on the radio. They also would play "rap shows or tapes" for about 35 minutes over the air. They always seem to play tapes around 4:00 AM, when the radio announcement would come on making everyone know you tapped it off the radio and it wasn't the official tape. *The World Famous Supreme Team* lasted for a while before it was replaced with a show called *Zulu Beats*. DJ Africa Islam and Donald Dee hosted the show. By the time *Zulu Beats* arrived on the air, I got hip on taping

48

the music low so my mom wouldn't hear the music upstairs. I thought you had to have the volume on high to make sure the tape was loud, but I was wrong. On my mom's stereo system, there was a record level. All I had to do was put the record level on 7 and have the volume barely on. The next morning I'd have a loud tape to play in school so everybody could hear all the new hip-hop music. *Zulu beats* also played live tapes from their Zulu nation parties. Everyone in the neighborhood knew I had tapes. They came to me to listen or trade. I would go uptown and to the Bronx more frequently to see friends and get tapes. Around this time I was claiming *Zulu Nation* on the down low. Zulu Nation is a hip hop organization founded by Afrika Bambaataa in the Bronx during the 1970's. Afrika Bambaataa is one of the three forefathers of the culture and music known as "Hip Hop". The Almighty Universal Zulu Nation has members in chapters all over the world. I picked up some black beads and read some of the Zulu lessons. I started hanging with some Zulu heads from school, going up to the Bronx River projects in Sound View on Tuesday afternoons with my man James from Laurelton, Queens. I had never been to Bronx River projects. I wasn't scared, but I was cautious. I didn't want people to think because I was from Queens I didn't know people or I didn't travel. But I met other Zulu brothers and it was pretty cool. Back in Queens, I started having trouble meeting anyone that was down with Zulu that was real. There were a lot of cats claiming Zulu but really weren't real. There was an overabundance of *"Peace Gods"* and saying I was down with Zulu wasn't something I needed to say if I wanted to remain safe. Zulunation was big in Manhattan and the Bronx but non-existent in Queens. While claiming Zulu during the day in school, I was still attending the kingdom hall at night. I prayed to God I didn't see anyone I knew from Zulu when I came knocking on a door offering the latest issues of the *Watchtower* and the *Awake*. By 1983, in the 10th grade I was all hip-hop during school, and down with the Jehovah Witnesses on Tuesday and Thursday night and all day Sunday. I started to feel confident with rapping after practicing in my basement for months. I really didn't write too much, basically freestyling. I was okay, decent for that time period. I would rhyme in the neighborhood to see what kind of responses I would receive. But I was nothing like this guy that rhymed that lived eight or nine blocks away, across Farmers Blvd. I had heard of him and his friends were cool with my friends. He called himself "Cool J" which stood for "Cool James". No one called him James, though. Instead people called him by his middle name, which is Todd. I had some friends that lived on the same block as him and we would play football in the street, rain or snow. When he talked he used a lot of big words I hadn't heard of before. My first impression of him was he must do well in English or be on the Honors Roll in school. We talked about whom we knew in the neighborhood, and come to find out we had a lot of friends in common. He knew all the neighborhood bullies and hard rocks and all the same corner cats I knew. He knew or heard about most of the girls on my side of Farmers Blvd, and vice versa. He was always playing demos and asking, "How's this sound?" and "Let me rewind this. Let me play it again. Tell me how I sound." You could tell he was determined and telling him he was good was definitely a motivation. He used to rhyme with this other guy we were cool with named Cal; his rap name was "Mello C". The talent in St Albans and Hollis, Queens was all over. It was just coming out the wood works and getting explosive. However, we just couldn't see how fast it was coming. You couldn't have convinced me "Cool J" (LL COOL J) would be one of the greatest emcees that ever touched a microphone. It was just fun to us, even when we took it seriously. The cool thing about my boy LL is that even after he started selling millions of records and winning accolades of awards, he was always around the way at his Grandmother's house still in the neighborhood kicking it with everyone he grew up with. After he released his second album with his love song, "I Need Love", he went into superstar status, and even inspired me to take this rap music more serious. I couldn't believe the type of money and fame he was getting. It was well deserved, and I'm very proud to have grown up with him.

There were others in the neighborhood getting noticed as well. Another childhood friend of mine that lived off of Farmers Blvd and 109th Avenue named Jeff was in the group called INTRO. He had a top selling single and an album on Atlantic records, but nothing after that. Queens was blowing up on the rap scene with Run-DMC, LL Cool J, Salt "N" Pepa, Kid N Play, and Kwame. I remember hearing tapes from parties in Manhattan and The Bronx and emcees would ask, "who is in the house?" and when it came to "Is Queens in the house?" there would be total silence. In 1984 I must say that Queens had come a long way. Unfortunately the drug scene in Queens also had come a long way.

Everyone was now hearing about hip-hop and hustling in Queens. The word was out about how cats in Queens were making some real money in the drug game, getting respected. Whatever was happening in Queens was also heard outside of Queens. The murder rate in Queens was going up. Cats all over Queens were getting street rich and super paid while dead bodies were piling up in the morgue. The New York City Police Department (NYPD) was doing more street patrol instead of just cruising in the car and trying to clean up the corners.

CHAPTER EIGHT: DOUBLE LIFE

I bought one of the biggest radios out at that time; it had a double cassette and an alarm system. It was crazy! My mom allowed me to have the radio but not take it outside at first because of the attention it drew. I brought it outside on the front steps at first, playing all my tapes and rocking the entire block. Some months later I rocked it out on Farmers Blvd. From then on I took it everywhere with me as long someone else helped me carry it. The radio got to be heavy after carrying it for 3-4 hours; and I had 10 tapes in my pocket to bump. When I took the radio to work, to the World Trade Center, I had a co-worker help me with it. When I took it to Long Island I had over 10 people with me. I took it with me to Queens Bridge Projects a couple of times, everywhere in the neighborhood. No one from the Kingdom Hall saw me with the radio, or knew I had it. My mother didn't say anything. Early '85 and I started going out to Long Island a lot more to date girls who were not from the Kingdom Hall. I started listening to a college radio station based out of Adelphi University. I found this radio station one Monday night after flipping the radio dial looking and this station called WBAU 90.3. At first, the radio channel was filled with static, but after I switched the knob to mono it was clear and banging. The radio DJ was named Mr. Bill and he was playing hip hop and Long Island rap demos, and sometimes the entire song of a record that contained a break-beat DJ's would cut up and mix on. One night the DJ played the entire songs for *"funky president"*, *"Fusion beat"*, *"Impeach the president"*, and *"Catch the Beat"*. I never heard these records in their entirety played on the radio, only just the break part. He also allowed dedications on the radio station from all over Long Island and Queens. People would call up and give shout outs to their peeps from around the way, whatever town they were from, or to whomever girl or guy you was dating at the time. I called up the radio station and I would speak to people who were part of the radio crew. I'd give my dedication no matter how long it was; I was representing Queens. At that time very few people from Queens were calling because they couldn't get the station on their radio. Some people from Queens were unaware of that radio station's broadcast airtime. I started giving shout outs to all my boys that went to the Hall, and all my neighborhood people. I felt good to hear my name on the airwaves several times during the radio show. I told my friends from the Kingdom Hall who weren't spiritual of course to listen for their shout outs and explained to them how to get the radio station to come in clear. Before you knew, the whole hood was listening. I was a senior in High School on the COOP work program. This allowed me to work one week and go to school the following week. I had to stay up on Monday nights until 1:00 AM, when the radio show was over. On Wednesday I would stay up until 4:00 AM because of the radio show "Zulu beats". I'd then have to get up at 7:00 AM for school or work, depending on the week. I was tired, but I had tapes for days. I had given enough shout outs that would have lasted for a month. I was getting my name out, and to me that was worth it. I was still attending the meetings at the Kingdom Hall, but not as consistently. I was a Wall Street Messenger for a company called First Boston, which was inside the World Trade Center. My hours were 9 to 5. I would get home around 6:45 PM, just enough time for the Tuesday night book study that started at 7:00 PM; and in time for the Thursday night meeting at 7:30 PM. It wasn't a problem until I told my mother that I would be doing overtime, getting off at 6:30 PM. I wouldn't get home until around 8:00 PM. I would miss the Tuesday night book study altogether and part of the Thursday meeting. That didn't sit well with my mother at all. I pushed it for a while but after several meetings being missed, my mother was livid and threatened to crack down. She stated that it would be in my best interest to get to the meetings by any means necessary, no matter what time I got there. So I started getting at the Tuesday night meeting around 7:35 PM, and the Thursday night meeting around 8:15 PM. My mother stated the only reason she allowed me to work was because I'd be making my own money to buy suits and shoes to wear in field service. Attending the meetings at the Kingdom Hall was a condition of working. I had to keep good grades in school to stay on the COOP program anyway, so grades didn't matter to my mother.

Sometimes I saw no benefit, missing a part or the entire meeting. If I could get away with going home I would. My mother saw what I was doing and took action. She started putting extra locks on the front and back doors. I couldn't get in unless she gave me the key, which she didn't. She also put bars on the windows upstairs and downstairs so I couldn't climb through. The only thing I did was pissed her off more with no choice but to go straight to the meetings after work. I couldn't get into the house, and whatever food she cooked I couldn't eat until she came home anyway. My mother would get me back for missing meetings by not allowing me to use the phone, making me stay in field service for four hours instead of two hours. She would clean up my room while I was at work and give all my "worldly" clothes to the goodwill that was up the street. To her, my leather jackets, my sheepskin, my leather pants, my sheepskin hat and anything that she deemed not fit to wear to the Kingdom Hall went to the goodwill. She even had the nerve to get my worldly friend that lived on my block to help her by taking my clothes to the goodwill and paid him! I came home one evening and all my leather and sheepskin items were gone! I asked my mother where my clothes were and she said, "I cleaned up your room and threw away all attire that wasn't fit to wear to the Kingdom Hall. I put it all in the goodwill box up the street." I ran outside and saw my friend that helped my mother. He told me my mother paid him to do it, but all my items should still be there in the goodwill. I ran down the street fast and went into the goodwill box and all my items were on the bottom. Thank goodness, because those leather and suede items were expensive and would have cost me a fortune to replace. My mother thought

I wouldn't be able to get my clothes back, but then I came back in the house with my clothes and smiling. My mother was pissed off. She would have to wait another day for payback.

When I was working on Wall Street as a messenger I was all over Manhattan delivering stocks and bonds. I was also coming across clothing and shoe stores, record stores, comic book stores, electronic stores, so I could find illegal microwave equipment to watch the UHF TV station Channel 69 back then in New York. One day I was in the 42nd Street area delivering stocks and I stopped to have something to eat. I went towards the subway station to go back downtown. I had subway tokens that were provided by my company, but I also had a C2 bus pass, which enabled me to ride the subway and the bus for free. I would keep the tokens for myself and use my train pass to enter the train station. I went through the gates and showed the clerk my pass. Suddenly, out of nowhere undercover New York City transit cops charged me and threw me against the wall. They went through my wallet and checked my pockets, pulling out my train pass. They wanted to know why I wasn't in school. I told them I was working this week and school next week. I showed them my Job ID but they said I looked too young to be working; and they never heard about a COOP program. They detained me for 30 minutes and called my boss at my job. Luckily he verified I was employed and verified my whereabouts in the 42nd street area delivering stocks. When kids used to cut class or school, 42nd street was the place to go. Having school truant cops in the area wasn't uncommon. I guess someone from the Kingdom Hall found it odd to see me in the 42nd street area as well and made a phone call to my mother. Brother Badstone, an Elder in the congregation, who just happens to be the father of one of my best friends, had nothing better to do but follow up on this offense and call my mother. When I get home my mother was annoyed and asked me, "Where were you today?" I answered, "I was at work today." She told me that Elder Badstone called her and he either heard or saw me around the 42nd Street vicinity during the day. She told me to be mindful of my surroundings. She really didn't care who saw me, as long as she knew where I was and what I was doing. This incident validated that my mother would back me up 100%, as long she knew what I was doing and where I was. She knew I was having sex, rapping in the streets, watching rated- R movies and even drinking. (I had smoked some weed but that didn't last long) It was almost like I was allowed a double life … to a certain degree. My mother would say she wanted me at a balance of half spiritual and half worldly. As far as she was concerned I was at all my meetings, I was on the Theocratic Ministry School giving bible talks, and in field service and going to school and working. Anything else was fine. I was going to roller skating rinks, local clubs, rapping at parties, working, hanging with worldly and kingdom halls kids. And I was doing well in high school. I had the latest clothes, jewelry, sneakers, shoes and (of course) GIRLS!!!!! Another incident that prompted attention from the Elders came about when I lent out my *Penthouse* magazine with nude photographs of then Mrs. America: Vanessa Williams. I had brought the magazine to the Assembly to show it off, and several of the Kingdom Hall kids from my congregation wanted to borrow it. The magazine went through several individuals; the last individual that saw the magazine was the son of a prominent Elder. Everybody knew that this guy, Halem, was destined for spiritual greatness. His father was grooming him to be an Elder or future district or circuit overseer, even bethel. The last thing he needed was for his son to be corrupt by me. Halem was actually a good kid and the grandson of Sister Brisler, who used to study the bible with my sister back in 1974. I even hung out with him at his house for a day when we were kids. Everyone could tell when he grew up, he would be a Jehovah Witness and he would be nothing less than an elder. When his mother found the magazine under the bed, my mother received another call about me. My mother already knew I bought the magazine, and she screamed on me! All I remember her saying was, "I told you not to be having' these Elders call me!" Before the elders came over to discuss this sexually graphic incident, my mother sat me down to go over what I was going to say and how to say it. My mother stated that I should say that the magazine wasn't for me but for my older brother who was living in Germany. The magazine wasn't available over in Europe and I bought it for him. He wasn't in the truth so it didn't matter why he wanted it. My mother said, "That's what you will tell the Elders when they get here." Three elders came over to my house and we all went into the living room. A prayer with Jehovah was done and then they asked me, "How I was doing?" I said, "Fine." One of the Elders started speaking about what was sexually unclean and about sexual pornographic material such as TV shows, radio, movies, and of course magazines. The Elders read several scriptures to me like Ephesians chapter 5 verses 1 thru 5 discussing uncleanness and of course 1 Corinthians 15:33 which states, "Bad association spoils useful habits". While one of the Elders was discussing the seriousness of sexual pornographic material with me, another Elder was pulling out the magazine from the briefcase. He pulled the magazine out slowly, like it was a deadly bomb. I was asked how I came across such a filthy magazine and how it got into the hands of precious Brother Brisler's son. I told them I gave the magazine to a certain individual and don't know how it got to Brother Brisler's son. I purchased the magazine in lower Manhattan from a newsstand for my older brother that wasn't in the truth and living in Germany. It would take months before this magazine would be available in Europe, so I bought it and was going to send it to Germany. I was asked by one of the Kingdom Hall kids if I had it and I said, "Yes." Instead of the magazine being in the mail, I brought the magazine to the assembly to show if off. I told them I was sorry about this offense and won't happen again and Satan must have made me stumble. They suggested I should read the scripture 1 Corinthians 15:33 out loud again. The Elders stated that in the future I should watch my association even in Jehovah's organization. I was told to avoid the world and not to be fooled by what the world offers. They told me to disassociate myself with individuals that's not seeking God's kingdom first, and that included family. We concluded with praying and my mother came out and to thank the Elders giving me the needed counsel. When they left, my mother just looked at me and said, "Do not have them come over my house again." I acknowledged, "I won't." I never had the Elders at my home again, despite living a double life that very few knew about. I just was a little more careful. My mother allowed this double life luxury and I took full advantage. If she said I didn't have to go to the Kingdom Hall anymore, I would have stopped going and kept doing what I was doing. I know some kids whose parents gave them the option to continue going to the Kingdom Hall or stop going when they turned 17 or 18. Some of my friends had that option and stopped going. When I talk to them now, the appreciation of knowing what's right and wrong is there, and going back to the Hall isn't something foreign. It might have been possible. However, their lifestyle still doesn't warrant them to dedicate their lives to Jehovah and get baptized. But the appreciation is still there. I have disfellowshipped friends who wish they had waited until they were more mature. They felt the pressure from family and friends who were "in the truth". The pressure was on the border of being forced or kicked out of their homes. They had to oblige or they would have been homeless. There were not a lot of options available for others and myself. It seemed to me that the organization only cared about how many publishers they had worldwide. I'm sure some kids were allowed to live a double life like myself, however, you won't hear about them writing a book. Then again they probably were in a better position to leave home or had an understanding parent or parents. I continued living a double life because I really had no choice. I was forced to have one type of life, but I wanted to experience and enjoy the other type of lifestyle, which was a worldly one regardless of what I was doing. When the time came to make a decision on which side of the fence I wanted to be on (the Jehovah side of the fence or the Satan side of the fence) ultimately it would have been my choice to make alone. I really can't say what choice I would've made if being forced by my mother wasn't an issue. I guess she was thinking that she would allow me to continue living a double life for a little longer, and then sometime down the road she would make the choice for me. She ended up doing that anyway.

CHAPTER NINE: BAD ASSOCIATION
SPOILS USEFUL HABITS

1 Corinthians 15:33 in the New World Translation of the Holy Scriptures are the most quoted. Anytime you were counseled by the brothers for any wrong doing, this scripture was definitely read. If you were just talking to someone "worldly", here comes a brother out of nowhere with a bible already opened to 1 Corinthians 15:33. You could cough wrong and you would hear, "Please, open up your bible to 1 Corinthians 15:33".

I kept balancing a double life. I didn't get too spiritual; I didn't get too worldly. At least that's what I thought. I was always with the girls trying to get numbers, or going outside of Queens to see them. I started traveling more outside of Queens to see girls all over the tri-state area. I didn't care where they lived as long as I was able to take a train or bus there. Everywhere I went I would tell people my name was "Geechie Dan" from Hollis, Queens. My name was traveling all around with respect to girls and on the hip-hop tip. I was in Long Island chasing girls and getting phone numbers from the college radio station WBAU 90.3 FM. My radio dedications were so many and so long that the people taking the phone requests were getting upset on having to read them all. I would be holding up the line with dedications, and trying to holler at the girls taking the messages. After several weeks of doing this, the DJ interning said, "Damn, Geechie. Why don't you just come up here and do your dedications yourself?" I said, "You haven't said anything but a thing," I asked for directions to get to Adelphi University in Garden City, Long Island where the radio station was located. The DJ was named Doctor Dre and he said, "Come on by Geechie." The timeslot for the radio show ran from 10:00 PM to 1:00 AM and was on Monday nights only. I went up to the radio station by myself, taking three buses and a long walk on a secluded road in the middle of the woods at night. When I finally got there I rang the buzzer and this guy named T came down to get me. He took me up on the elevator to a floor where there were people all over the place having a great time and chillin'. I met everyone from the show! I met Mr. Bill, who I was originally listening to before Doctor Dre. Mr. Bill was mentoring Doctor Dre to take over his slot. Mr. Bill was graduating college, and moving on to the next phase in the music business. I was finally putting the faces with the voices I was hearing on the radio. Since my dedications were lengthy, I started writing them and saying them myself over the air. I started to work the phones and take dedications from other callers, mostly girls all over Nassau and Suffolk Counties. Nobody told me to answer phones or paid me to do this. I did this for the love of hip-hop, and the love I had for the people at the radio station because they showed me mad love. I got along with everybody that was associated with the station. I had no hang ups about anything. It felt good to be part of something that I liked and chose to be a part of, unlike the Kingdom Hall. As I was taking their dedications and requests, I was getting their phone numbers. If they sounded fly over the phone I was getting the number, no question. I was getting a lot of listeners from Queens to call up and represent. I told them to tell their friends to listen on Monday nights to the show. It was free advertising for me and for the radio station. My week was getting hectic from working, school, going to the radio station on Monday nights, going to the book study on Tuesday night, taping Zulu beats on Wednesday night, going to the Thursday night meeting and traveling Friday night and Saturday to see all the girls I just met from the radio station. I was doing all this traveling to Long Island and Queens on the bus. I still had to do my homework and go to field service on Sunday, along with attending the Sunday meeting. I used the radio station as an avenue to get my name out and meet girls. However, I started meeting too many girls. I would meet girls and once I said my name, they would know I was with the radio station. I was getting labeled as a player. I met some more people associated with the radio station and they were called the "Spectrum City Crew". They all were from Long Island and had their own collection of DJ's, emcees, rap crews, promoters, producers, and had their own unique sound of hip hop. To hear how these brothers got down with their sound coming from Long Island was like hearing a Cold Crush 4 tape for the first time. You knew it was different and in a class of its own. It was still hip-hop but it didn't have that grimy urban element I was so used to hearing with the Bronx hip-hop. That's the beauty of hip-hop. It's not supposed to sound the same. Two individuals of the radio station stood out immediately as soon as I met them. The first individual was actually a student at the college and a member of Spectrum City. When I heard him speak I knew he was ahead of his time. He was like a fiery trouble maker with words and that he was willing to go all out on the intellect. I really didn't know how to read him at first, and his rap name just didn't fit how he talked. His rap name then was "Chuckie D". It sounded like a name for someone else other than him. It reminded me of a name for a kid rapper. I didn't want to call him "Chuckie", like he was a little kid. I just called him by his real name, which was Chuck. There was this other brother I met hangin' with Chuck that reminded me of myself. He was hilarious, a fool to the extreme. But he had a serious side to him; he showed me mad love. He was the ultimate nut in Long Island and went by the weirdest but most unique name. His name was Flavor. He was a DJ and an emcee respectfully. I've met some individuals with personalities but Flavor was just how his name was. FLAVOR! I met most of the crews that were making demos for the radio station and they showed me love. I even did a freestyle rap with a rap crew from Freeport, Long Island. Rapper Biz Markie was doing the human beat box over the freestyle. I still have the tape to this day. No one knew I was going to the Kingdom Hall, and I didn't mention it.

CHAPTER TEN: 1985

I was giving bible talk-2 at the Theocratic Ministry School every 4 months. I was trying to get out of giving talks but it only made my mother tighten up her grip on me. I just had to continue living a double life. I was having sex regularly with many girls, and I wasn't feeling shameful nor was I about to brag to anyone from the Hall. I was at the radio station WBAU on Monday nights and my name was out there in the streets. I was making money working on Wall Street and I was about to graduate high school. I was drinking and partying, doing everything I wanted at a balance. I graduated high school in June of 1985. I had to take a summer class for 2 credits to get my High School Diploma in August. I went to summer school at Jamaica High School and continued working over the summer. I was also supposed to be receiving paperwork for my guardianship account. The court appointed my mother over the account until I turned 18. I would then be able to receive my money that was set up from my father's death. I never saw the paperwork, and no money was received. I asked my mother about it and she stated, "There was no more money. It was already used to fix up the house when our house caught on fire some years ago." An Elder by the name of Brother James sometimes came by the house to check on me and see where he could help me spiritually. He came at me in a sincere way, like he wanted to make sure I was heading on to the right path. He was doing fine with his daughters, but his 2 sons gave him his own demons but he still seemed sincere. My mother didn't trust him, however. I was turning 18 years old in August, and Brother James was there to encourage me to do my lawful duty and register for the Armed Forces, required by all males at 18. As long as the Government laws did not conflict with Jehovah laws, I was in good standing in the eyes of Jehovah and my mother. So, I registered and received my card confirming my registration in the Armed Forces. I also received some counseling from the scriptures about the Armed Forces and why we don't believe in serving our country, or any country for that fact. If I wanted to join the Armed Forces I couldn't be a Jehovah's Witness. I was seeing Brother James more frequently in my paths. He was persistent in having a bible study with me. This delighted my mother to the point where she thought I was getting serious about the truth. My Sundays were now occupied all day, starting with the Sunday morning meeting. I then had Sunday afternoon field service, my bible study with Brother James, my homework and then housework. Thankfully, there were six more days out of the week to play. In the fall of 1985, my COOP job with First Boston ended. I started working at Lazard Freres, an investment firm located at One Rockefeller Plaza. I was working in the supply room. I also had received my first car, which was a 1979 Cadillac Seville. I started York Community College in Jamaica, Queens. I was working a new job, had a new car and started dating one of the girls I met over the summer from Six Flags amusement park in New Jersey, traveling back and forth to the Bronx to see her. I also met one of my best friends at my new job. His name was Keith. I didn't tell him about the Kingdom Hall, and didn't care to share it with anyone at my new job. Telling people I went to the Kingdom Hall was like telling people I was in a secret organization. I was already living a double life, so any conversation about me attending the Kingdom Hall would just add fuel to the fire. And I wasn't up for any discussions and be viewed as a full-fledge Jehovah Witness standing up for my organization. In reality I was just a follower based off association. I just had to be careful in my double living, because as soon as I got caught doing something wrong in the Kingdom Hall, it would be, *"That's Sister Chamberlayne's son."* And my mother did not want another incident involving me. I felt like I had to defend Jehovah's Witnesses as a religion and everything they stood for even though I wasn't one. Just because my mother made me go to the Kingdom Hall that didn't necessarily mean I believed in everything the organization stood for. When it came to someone asking me about celebrating my birthday, or someone else's birthday, I felt like a birthday should be recognized and observed. I just didn't think anyone should go overboard with the celebrating, and should just enjoy their day. It didn't matter too much to me about birthdays back then because I felt I already missed more of a decade of my own. The reason why Jehovah's Witnesses don't celebrate birthdays is because they believe the custom of celebration of birthdays is from ancient, false religions. Supposedly, the early Christians never celebrated their birthdays and true Christians shouldn't celebrate them now. The celebration of Thanksgiving didn't stop when my mother got baptized, however. My mother and I never stopped celebrating Thanksgiving. There are a lot of Witnesses that celebrate Thanksgiving, whether it's done on Thursday on Friday. Christmas is another holiday Jehovah Witnesses are not supposed to celebrate because the bible doesn't mention December 25th as Jesus Christ's birthday; according to them. However, a Christmas bonus isn't turned down. If a holiday were convenient to celebrate, it would be celebrated. The only holidays my mother and I celebrated together while attending the kingdom hall were Thanksgiving and the Memorial. The Memorial is the celebration of Jesus Christ's death and not his birth. It's similar to the Christian holiday, Easter; however the organization celebrates Jesus Christ's death differently. When the Memorial would occur, the Kingdom Hall would be packed. If it got too crowded the men would give their seat up so the women would be comfortably seated. The front of the Kingdom Hall, near the stage was a table filled with bottles of un-fermented wine and unleavened bread, which is bread that doesn't have any yeast. The opening to the celebration starts off with a song and a prayer welcoming everyone in attendance to celebrate this joyous occasion and the significance of it. The significance of the celebration would be talked about with the scriptures that supported it. This included the reading of the books of Matthew, Mark, Luke and John. This celebration is recognized by Jehovah Witnesses all over the world, on the same evening. The organization also reports how many people were in the attendance, and how many individuals partook from the wine and bread. Anyone who drank some wine and ate a piece of bread were part of the "Anointed Class" and were considered a part of the heavenly class of 144,000 that were going to rule with Jesus Christ in heaven. Remember the zealous Sister Mintz woman that used to watch me? I mentioned her earlier in the book about her being "one of the anointed". She wasn't in our congregation but all the witnesses had heard and saw her partake in the wine and bread. The Congregation would keep in account who partook in the celebration and reported this back to the Society. Every year, every one in the congregation including myself got excited to see and observe who partook in this celebration and who the individuals were that were going to heaven. There wouldn't be anyone to do this in our congregation until the mid 80's. It was a Sister that my mother and I had known for years who drank from the wine and ate the bread. It would be something to gossip about until we saw the next person to partake in the celebration. After the celebration, the singing of the song was done and then the prayer for the conclusion of the celebration. In the coming months the Society would tell the figures of how many were in attendance and who partook in the celebration. Everyone would applaud because the numbers would be in the millions. The organization used these figures of how many Jehovah Witnesses were all over the world, even though this figure included people that were not Witnesses but were invited to the celebration by Witnesses.

My mother saw how busy I was with work, college, attending the meetings, conducting bible studies, and having my own bible study. On top of all that I had field service and still found time for hanging out at the radio station and being with my new girlfriend from the Bronx. But things started to fall apart in my mother's eyes. First, and most importantly, my girlfriend and I started to get close. I was in the Bronx at least two times a week, mostly Friday and

Saturday. Sunday through Thursday was out. Sunday was dedicated to my Kingdom Hall activities, and Monday night was the radio station. Tuesday and Thursday nights were the meetings and Wednesday night was school. My girlfriend and I were having sex like rabbits and we couldn't stop. I don't know if it was lust or my first love but all I knew is I had gone from going to the Bronx two times a week to four times a week. I was going to York College on Wednesday nights. After awhile, I dropped out. I didn't tell my mother. On Wednesday nights I went straight to the Bronx after work. I would stay in the Bronx until 10:00 PM then head back to Queens, getting home around 11:15 PM. I would also attend an early meeting on Sunday so I could go the Bronx on Sunday afternoon.

It was winter. I remember calling a cab to pick me up at Evergreen Avenue in the Sound View section of the Bronx where my girlfriend lived, taking the cab to Westchester Ave where I had to catch the Q44 bus back to Queens. If I missed the bus, I would have to wait for another hour for another one. I was missing the Tuesday night book study by telling my mother I was working late and doing over time. I was also meeting other DJ's and rappers that were making demos for the radio station. I was telling my mother that I had a chance to make a demo for the radio station, a possibility for getting a recording contract. I met this DJ named Shaun who lived in Flushing and he already had an emcee but I wanted him to help me make a demo for the radio station. My mother started to get angry because I was missing the Tuesday night book study. I told her that I wanted to make a record like the guy in our neighborhood "Cool J". I already had a lightweight following from my name in the neighborhood and from being on college radio, where she sometimes heard my name being mentioned. She saw that the radio station was all about fun and there wasn't any profanity. She had met some of the guys from the radio station and wasn't too receptive at first but I assured her I would attend the Thursday and Sunday meetings. I would do all the demo stuff at DJ

Shawn's house after work on Monday. I now had five days with my girl and one day for my rap demo. I picked the samples I wanted and gave them to my DJ. We looped it and then he added the chorus and I added my lyrics. I didn't even write the lyrics, I just went off my head. After three Mondays of working on the song, I took it up to the radio station and told Doctor Dre to play it. He checked it to make sure it was nothing crazy. It was my first demo song called *"Lets Dance"*. I told everyone I knew to be on the lookout for my song and to record it. Doctor Dre played the song and everyone loved it. The people from my neighborhood were requesting my song; they thought it was a whole record and started saying, "That's Geechie Dan's record!" In reality it was just a demo for the radio station. I played it for my mother and she was happy to hear I was enjoying something I wanted to do. She opened up a little and gave me her blessing on this "rap thing" since she knew "Mr. Cool J" (as she called LL) was already successful and from the same neighborhood. LL Cool J was already on TV and magazine covers, Soul train, Award Shows and telling the world on how he started out with his grandparents buying him recording equipment. My mother really was excited when LL Cool J's DJ came to my house with my friends. I already knew Philpot (as we called him) but I wanted him to meet my mother. Meeting him reassured her that this guy wasn't any hip-hop criminal. The following Sunday meeting, there was a talk given by Elder James regarding the organizations viewpoint on having a music career. While discussing this topic, Brother James kept looking at me whenever he referenced rappers and rap music. He was getting the names of rappers mixed up by saying, "We have individuals in the Christian Congregation that want to be like RUN-*DMQ* and *Cool Ray*." I smirked and laughed when he got the names wrong. I wasn't stupid. I knew he was talking about me. He was looking straight at me. I didn't care if he was talking about me or not, I had just made another demo for the radio station called *"Outstanding"* which was a recorded loop of the record *"Outstanding"* by the Gap Band. The only difference was I had rapped over the break part. I was still getting response on my first demo and even had a well-known street rapper from Queens call up the radio station and say he liked it and I need to check him out. I had heard of this rapper for some years but never met him. This rapper was one of the best freestyle and battle rappers I ever heard. To have him call up the radio station and say he liked my songs was very encouraging. He told me to take the Q5 bus to Merrick Blvd and 219th street in Laurelton, Queens and go to his mom's house. I was to meet him at Poppa Kim's grocery store on Merrick Blvd and 229th street and ask for "Mikey D." I was looking for someone at least 6'2" in height with dark skin, black and rough looking. Instead, this skinny light skin guy met me with green eyes in front of the store. He was my height, and had 10 to 15 friends with him. He was drinking beer and rhyming his ass off. The only other person I heard rhyming on this level was LL Cool J. I didn't think I would ever hear someone rhyme like he did. This guy was a rhyme beast in the illiest sense. I went over to him and I said, "Yo, you Mikey D?" He looked at me and said, "You Geechie Dan?" I said, "Yeah. What's up?" He gave me a bear hug and introduced me as emcee Geechie Dan from Hollis. He told his crew that I was down with the WBAU radio crew in Long Island. He gave me a beer and we all walked up and down Merrick Blvd, free styling and rhyming all night. This guy was rapping like *all night* and wouldn't stop! I mentioned to him how much he reminded me of Cool J from around my way. He said, "Oh Todd, I used to rhyme with him. I gave him the LL name for *Ladies Love.*" I didn't know then if that was true but it was confirmed by LL in his autobiography back in 1997. We walked all over Queens drinking Ole, English malt liquor. We finally arrived at his girlfriend's crib, located at Rochdale in Jamaica, Queens. He introduced me to her and her sister and their mother. I received mad love from them. He had record singles that were playing on the radio, and he was on a record label called "Public Records." He gave me the phone number and name of the owner, prompting me to call him because he might like the demos I made for the radio station. I called him and set up a meeting. He lived off of Broadway, not far from Central Park. I went into his building where the doorman rang me up to his apartment. I walked in and he shook my hand nervously. I sat down and took out my demos. He played *"Lets Dance"* first and loved it. It was a rough version; I didn't even write down the lyrics. He talked about his new label and what artists he had signed. He had signed "Mikey D", and emcee "Special K" from the rap group *The Treacherous 3,* who were on Sugar Hill records. He stated he liked *"Lets Dance"* and stated I should use it as a single and said I needed to record it at a professional studio. He said to call him when I was ready. He presented two contracts. One contract was for me and the other contract was for DJ Shawn who was helping me. I was so happy; I could have walked back to Queens. I was reading the recording contract on the subway heading up towards the Bronx to my girlfriend's house. We celebrated and talked about what car I wanted, where I wanted to live and how I would try to remain humble. I was acting like I had a million dollar deal. When I got home I told my neighborhood peeps and everyone was happy for me. Then I told my mother about the meeting and I showed her the recording contract. She acted happy but I knew she wasn't. She asked in a concern voice, "Sweetie, has a lawyer looked at this yet?" I answered half-heartedly, "Not yet." In the back of my mind I was hoping it was the perfect contract to allow me to leave home and buy my own house. I took the contract to an entertainment lawyer in Flushing, Queens. The lawyer took one look at it and laughed while throwing it right back to me. The only thing I was looking at was the $1500.00 signing bonus I was getting after I signed it. I asked him, "Why are you laughing? This isn't a joke." He looked into my eyes and sternly said, "I charged a certain amount of dollars to look over REAL RECORDING CONTRACTS and not bullshit contracts like the one you just handed me." He looked at the first page of the recording contract and said, "You are wasting my time." He took a red pen and started making corrections. He stated one last time, "If you sign this, you looking to get ripped off." The contract was so bad he didn't even bother charging me. I gave the other contract to DJ Shaun and he declined signing as well. It was a bad deal all around. Then reality set back in and I realized I wasn't leaving home any time soon, and I was still going to the Kingdom Hall. My mother won again. However, I wasn't going to give up that easily. After the contract fiasco, my mother began tightening her grip of control on me. My days living a double life were about to be slowed down and eventually stopped. My mother saw I wasn't being consistent with attending the Tuesday night meeting. She viewed my girlfriend and rapping as a distraction. She began plotting and planting the seed to get rid of my girlfriend in the Bronx. First she invited my girlfriend to come to Jamaica, Queens and meet her for lunch. My girlfriend was instructed to take the Q44 bus to the last stop in Queens where my mother would be waiting. My mother wanted to meet the girl who was taking up my time and keeping me away from the meetings.

My girlfriend naively thought the invitation was a nice gesture on my mother's part. She believed my mother was opening up, and being sincere. Once my mother gained her trust, she invited her to a Sunday meeting. I was angry! I didn't want my girlfriend to attend the Kingdom Hall. I picked up my girlfriend early Sunday morning to take her to Queens for the meeting. My mother knew I wanted to be with my girlfriend, but she also was hoping my girlfriend wouldn't want to be bothered with me once she witnessed the goings-on of the Kingdom Hall. The seed was planted and I didn't have a clue. My friend Keith was always weary of anything my mother was involved in. He laughed when I told him my mother had invited my girlfriend to the Sunday meeting. I told Keith how my mother was starting becoming more controlling, and he asked me, "Why do you still go to the Kingdom Hall?" I answered, "If I don't go I'll have to live somewhere else. Plus my mom was appointed my guardian over the guardianship account that my father left me. I was supposed to receive it at 18, and I don't really understand the status of it. I didn't receive any certified mail from the Surrogate's Court or any phone calls. I guess it

Daniel J. Chamberlayne

was all spent." My friend Keith stated, "You better look into that, kid." I asked my mother again and she said, "There isn't any money left from your trust at this time. Most of the money was used for your private schooling and to fix up the house from the first fire. There is enough to get you a vehicle from the auction and maybe some money will be available when you turn 21. I'll put the house in your name so you will always have a home." It was no coincidence that the mortgage on our house in Hollis, Queens was paid off around the same time I turned 18. I wasn't thinking that my mother would do anything deceitful, at least not against me. After all, she was my mother. Why would I think anything different? After some years of investigating and making phone calls, I finally found out what happened with my guardianship money. It wasn't pretty; it was illegal and all done in the name of Jehovah.

CHAPTER ELEVEN: MY MOTHER USES THE ORGANIZATION TO CRUSH MY FIRST LOVE

It was the spring of 1987 and I was still with my girlfriend in the Bronx, despite pressure from my mother. Seeing my girlfriend in addition to all the meetings was starting to get hectic. We were having sex a lot more and found myself getting whipped with lust while traveling back and forth from Queens to the Bronx. The Q44 bus was turning into my second home. I started missing meetings and spending all my money and time in the Bronx. My mother began locking me out of the house. My incessant knocking and ringing got so bad it would wake up the neighbors. Some nights, around 1:00 in the morning, I would be kicking, knocking and punching the door. It would be cold and raining, but my mother wasn't budging. She would be on the phone in her cozy bedroom with two heaters with her bedroom door closed just chilling and laughing on the phone. She figured since I wanted to be out all night, I might as well stay out for the whole night. There were many nights I slept on the front steps or in the back of her car. Sometimes she would come downstairs and open the door to let me in depending on the time. If it was after 1:00 AM, I was sleeping outside no matter what the weather or temperature was. I made it my business to leave the Bronx no later than 10:00 PM so I could get home by 11:45 PM. I had dropped out of York College but I was still going to the radio station on Monday night. I brought my homeboys KB and Tim with me most of the time. Sometimes I brought my girlfriend and her friends. Doctor Dre told me, "You more than welcome to come up to the radio station, but don't be bringing the whole neighborhood with you." I was allowed to drive my car to attend the meetings, but as soon as I started missing meetings, the car would be in the driveway blocked by my mother's car. My mother did this often when I was involved with worldly people or activity. I had to drop my

73

worldly friends off down the street and clean up the car from beer bottles and weed scent, put in new fresheners, and empty out the ashtrays. My mother was trying to make a profound statement that she was tired of me missing meetings and spending all my time in the Bronx. She was determined to keep pressure on me even if it resulted in me calling the police on her. I was tired of playing this game after several months of getting locked out in the cold. One night the temperature was below 20 degrees and I was freezing and my mother wouldn't let me in. I was kicking and screaming to get inside. My mother was right in the kitchen by the stove smiling, not caring whether or not I froze. I think one of my neighbors called the police after hearing me kick and scream for over an hour. Eventually a cop car pulled up in front of my house, lights flashing and two cops got out. I immediately told them I lived at the house because I knew how NYPD got down. Shoot to kill and ask questions later. I explained that I was trying to get into my house but my mother wasn't trying to open the door and let me in. They asked me, "Why would your mother lock you out? Are you a criminal or on drugs? Did you just get out of jail?" I said, "No," telling them that I was coming home from my girlfriend's house in the Bronx. I even said I was a rapper that just received a record deal. I continued that I was in college, working at an investment firm in midtown Manhattan. I told them that I was going to the Kingdom Hall and my mother was angry that I was missing meetings as of late. The cop asked, "And your mom is doing this to you?" He continued in a disbelieving manner, "I find it hard to believe that your mother is doing this just because you missed a few meetings. There must be something going on that you're not telling us." My mother looked out and saw me with the police. She unlocked the door and let us in. My mother glared at me. I knew I was in for it once the police left. She quickly put on her innocent game face while greeting the officers in an annoying, polite, nonchalant manner. The police explained that a neighbor called about a disturbance next door. The cops inquired why I was being locked out, especially if I was a good kid ... according to what I told

74

them. My mother smirked and laughed, "What lie did he tell you?" I quickly got defensive and said, "Why are you doing this to me?" I started crying and saying, "I'm not doing anything wrong! I always do what you want me to do but it's never enough." The police instructed me to calm down and to go outside while they talked to my mom. I stood outside in front of my house for 10 or 15 minutes. I saw some people that lived on my block that were on their way home. After seeing the cop cars and flashing lights they asked, "Is everything ok, Geechie?" I said, "Yeah, you know the usual, my moms locking me out again."

"For real?"

"Yeah.I was making' so much noise trying to get in that the neighbors called the cops."

"Damn. Sorry, man."

"Ain't nothing', it's the usual."

After while one of the cops came outside and said, "We talked to your mom and got her side of the story. She really doesn't like you coming home from the Bronx at this time of the night. She'll let you back in the house, but she wants you to start attending the Kingdom Hall meetings regularly." The police continued sympathetically, "You sound like you have a promising future ahead of you. Your mother shouldn't be so hard on you but she's just concerned." The police advised, "Don't say anything to upset her. Tell your mom that you love her and go straight to bed." The officer patted me on my back and said, "Other than what's happened, have a good night, kid. Remember, layoff from going to the Bronx so much." I assured him that I would. I then thanked both officers for helping me get back in my house. I rushed inside to do as the cop instructed, but my mother locked the door from behind me and said, "Don't you think just because the police came that this is over."

I said nothing, just as the cop instructed. I couldn't even squeeze out *'I love you'*. I went to my room, turned on the heater, and got my dress clothes ready for work in the morning. I went to bed wondering what my mother had told those police officers.

The next day, I went to work and saw Keith. I told him what happened and he laughed, "Yo, your moms ain't no joke." I called my girlfriend from work and told her what happened. She mentioned that my mom wasn't feeling her. She suggested I chill on coming up to the Bronx so much. She suggested that we see each other on the weekends. My girlfriend didn't want to be the cause of me getting kicked out of my house. She knew my mother was adding a lot of pressure on me because of our relationship.

Another devious plot my mother concocted was allowing me to have a 'gathering', which is a party; the organization just doesn't like calling it a party. But that's what it is. I asked if my friends could come and my mother answered, "Sure sweetie." Her smile screamed SUCKER! But I didn't notice it. I was too busy planning the gathering. The catch was that I could only invite my Kingdom Hall friends. But my mom did allow me to invite my girlfriend. The gathering would be in the afternoon, after the Sunday meeting. My mother promised to make her famous Lasagna and Pepper Steak and all my favorite foods (which is anything and everything edible). I thought this was great. My girlfriend could finally meet the rest of my Kingdom Hall peeps other than Tim and Joe. I only invited the kids from my congregation that were cool not the ones that were too spiritual. The last thing I needed was for them to see my worldly girlfriend and start holding court with their rigid parents. I also didn't want my girlfriend to be uncomfortable. When Sunday came I knew it was going to be a day I would never forget. I didn't think it was going to be a disaster, a day of holy hell. It started out as the usual getting up for Sunday morning meeting, the watchtower meeting, and an hour in field service for the afternoon. All my peeps were coming over around 4:00. I was going to help my mother cook and prepare the food, set the table and the other housework. The first to show up were my man Anthony and his pretty sister who I always had a crush on. Then my man Tim and Joe came through; behind them I saw Sister Marie coming through the gate. She was smiling and so happy to attend my gathering. She was an elderly sister, not a peer of mine. I was courteous as she slowly walked in the house. She needed help walking despite having a cane. I said, "Hi, Sister Marie. What a surprise to see you here." I looked dead at my mother in disgust now realizing that she was setting me up. I said to my mother, "I thought this gathering was for me and my friends." My mother told me, "This gathering is for you and the friends." Her words rattled me, especially the tone in which she emphasized *and the friends*. I asked Tim to come with me to the Bronx to pick up my girlfriend. I tried to remain calm but I was too busy trying to figure out whom else my mother invited to this so-called gathering of' mine. As I was leaving the front entrance of my house, more of the 'friends' were pulling up to the house, parking their cars. I looked at my friend Tim and said, "Let's get the hell out of here!" When Tim and I got to my girlfriends, she was so hurt that my mother would pull a stunt like this, though not surprised. I told my girlfriend to get into the car and that we were heading back to Queens. We pulled up to my house where there were cars everywhere. All the Witnesses that were at the Sunday meeting were now at my house. There were Elders, older women, publishers and kids … hell damn near the whole congregation was at my house. When the witnesses saw my girlfriend, it was like feeding time at the zoo, and she was the raw food for the lions. The witnesses ran over to her and started asking her a million questions about where she lived. They wanted to know if she went to the Kingdom Hall, if she'd like a bible study, had she ever gone to the Kingdom Hall and why was she my girlfriend?

There were all sorts of questions. They surrounded her, trying to see who would be the one to get a bible study commitment. I saw my mother in the kitchen, smirking. I went to confront her. We started yelling at each other in the kitchen and I ran outside. My girlfriend came out and saw me crying. "I hate her!" I screamed between sobs. "She had this planned all along!" After my girlfriend calmed me down and regained my composure, we went back inside and avoided my girlfriend to show the witnesses I had self-control. My house was full of Jehovah Witnesses that I didn't invite. My gathering wasn't fun at all. I told my real peoples I would see them again, on the rebound or I'd call them to apologize for not being a perfect host. But they understood the circumstances. I told everyone that I hoped they had a great time and enjoyed the food. But underneath I was upset at what my mother had done to my girlfriend. I was determined that this premeditated scheme wasn't going to be successful. I told my friend Tim that I was taking my girlfriend home, and I'd stop by his house later. On the drive to the Bronx my girlfriend and I talked about how foul my mother was. We agreed that this had all been planned to break us up. Sadly my girlfriend stated, "Well, it worked." She didn't think she could deal with it anymore. However, if we kept seeing each other, the pressure that my mother was putting on me would triple. My girlfriend didn't want to see me go through this anymore. Her mother had suggested on numerous occasions that I live with them in their two-bedroom apartment. It would have been my girlfriend and I in one room and her mother and her mother's boyfriend in another. I was seriously considering it. My mother would have found some way to make sure that wouldn't happen. My girlfriend saw something like this from my mother coming, but like everybody else, she didn't want to go head-to-head with my mother. It would have been like hitting a brick wall. You were going to lose. Everyone felt sorry for me, but at the end of the day, they would rather it be I than them. It wasn't worth the headaches. We broke up that Sunday evening, and I cried like a baby on the drive home. This was my first love and after 8 months, we weren't going to be together anymore. My mother used the congregation to do this and show me who was in control. The pressure was turned up to a level I had never experienced. She was determined to make me become a Jehovah Witness, even if it meant using deception, bribery and fear. The days of my mother allowing me to continue living a double life were gone. "The former things have passed away." (Rev 21:4).

Little Daniel at 6 at Father's job at JFK international airport

Daniel's baptism pictures, September 4, 1988, Circuit Assembly in Jersey City, NJ

Daniel J. Chamberlayne

Inside of a Kingdom Hall in the early 1980s

CHAPTER TWELVE: YOU BETTER GET BAPTIZED OR ELSE

With my girlfriend no longer in the picture, my mother was now able to manipulate and prep me for dedication and baptism. I had to ask: *Why is my mother so* gun-ho *about me becoming a Jehovah Witness?* Just a couple of years ago, she wasn't the most spiritual person, but it appeared (and I stress *appeared*) that she was getting more zealous about her spirituality as the years went on. But she wasn't fooling me. Maybe she was fooling the congregation by visiting different "friends" in other congregations and visits to Watchtower Farms and Printing facilities all over world. My mother had Jehovah's Witness friends all over the world. She would visit France, Germany, Canada, Bogotá, South America, and Sydney, Australia. My mother was in Sydney, Australia when she missed the District Convention. The nursing patient she was taking care of required 24-hour assistance. There were two District Assemblies left in the world, one in Mexico and another in Sydney, Australia. She did not want to return to Mexico, for obvious reasons. So she went to Australia. When "the friends" heard about this they thought only someone strong and sincere in the "truth" that loved Jehovah and his people greatly, would do this. Many wondered how she was able to afford it. The airline costs were close to $2000.00, which she paid with one of her airline credit cards. My mother claims she took the matter to Jehovah in prayer and was blessed. Her 90 hours of field ministry per month as a regular full time pioneer was making a profound statement that she was giving Jehovah and the organization her all. In the organization eyes, she was no longer "weak in the truth" or a "babe of the truth" and it fooled many, including myself. I always thought my mother was too slick to be spiritual so the possibility of her being spiritual couldn't be serious. She now had to uphold this new spiritual "act." The next thing left was for me to follow suit. There were other teenagers with situations similar to mine only they had to deal with their entire family pressuring them. My mother wanted me to get more spiritual. The first thing she had me do was comment more at the *Watchtower* meetings. I always knew the answers at the *Watchtower* meetings but felt compelled to keep them to myself. I didn't want to give the perception I was getting spiritual, even though it wasn't rocket science material. However, that was about to change.

My mother wanted the comments I made to be long comments with a scripture from the bible to back it up. She started bragging about how smart I was, and how I was good at studying and knowing all the answers at the meetings. She would say, "You are so smart, sweetie. You know Bible verses so well, and you're able to explain things better than me." However I knew what she was trying to do.

For encouragement my mother would offer ten or fifteen dollars for each comment I made at the *Watchtower* meetings. The comments made had to be at least 30 seconds long and cross-referenced with a scripture in the Bible. I looked at my mother like she was crazy, refusing at first. But after a few elbows to my ribs, I would raise my hand to comment. My mother would look at me smiling and say, "That's good sweetie." As time went on, the price went up to twenty-five and thirty dollars per comment. For that price, my comments would require at least 2 scriptures mentioned or cross-referenced. My comments had to be straight to point. I made it difficult for people to comment after me; we would just have to move on to the next paragraph. From the comments I was making, the congregation just knew my mother was doing a great job with me. I was a step closer to dedication and baptism. I hated how my mother could bribe me. And like a dummy I'd go for it. It would be something I'd regret but hey, like pretty boy blue...I just needed the money. Once she had me in her pocket, it was smooth sailing from there; my mom could get away with anything, including throwing cold water on me on Sunday mornings to get me up for the Sunday service. I would still rap and hang out on Saturday nights coming home at 4:00 AM. My mother figured if I could hang out all night, I could get my butt up for Sunday service. I would explain to my mother I had no problem going to the Sunday meetings, however getting up at 8:45 in the morning and staying awake at the meetings would be putting my ribs in trouble. (My mother would poke me in my ribs whenever I was falling asleep). I suggested to my mother that after getting some sleep, I would go to another congregation that had their Sunday meetings in the afternoon. She thought it was a good idea until she noticed I wasn't commenting at the *Watchtower* meetings anymore. I just didn't feel comfortable making comments at another congregation's *Watchtower* meetings. Going to other congregations didn't last long. It was quickly back to Sunday mornings at my congregation and throwing cold water on me to get me up. My mother would call up to me at first. Then when that wasn't working she resorted to clicking the attic light on and off. And when that still didn't work, she would come upstairs to my room with a pot full of cold water and throw it over me. It would leave my bed and I soaking wet. She would say while laughing, "I bet your ass will get up now!" I had no choice but to get up and dry myself off in the bathroom. I thought about all the places I wanted to travel to with my car instead of going to the Sunday meeting. But I wasn't going anywhere with my car blocked in. I used to get up on Sunday mornings to empty out the ashtrays, take out any beer bottles and make sure it smelled okay. I'd do all of this the night before, but developed a habit of double-checking. My mother made me pick up several older sisters that didn't have a ride to the meetings. I had to make sure the back seats were fine. Once I finished getting dressed, I would go pick up her girlfriends and come back to the house and wait for her. Then all of us would proceed to the Kingdom Hall. I would hear comments from the older sisters while they were in the back of the car saying, *"What a beautiful car you have."* and *"Sister Chamberlayne, you have such a wonderful and handsome son. He has grown up so fast and so tall."* Once the meetings were over, I would have to take all the older sisters back home, and then find out where "the group" was meeting for the afternoon field service. After in field service and Bible study, I would have my car to myself for the rest of the Sunday evening. This was the only way I was going to be able to drive my car. The pressure was building up so much that my mother was hinting that I should conduct a bible study with Sister Bosh's husband, Matt. He wasn't "in the truth" but had questions about "the truth". If a study came out of it, it was going to be with me and me alone. He liked the way I carried myself when visiting. He heard from my mother that I was able to explain certain Bible scriptures very well. He admired that because I was so young. Sister Bosh and her husband had a teenage daughter who was getting herself into a little trouble with boys. Her father suggested I talk to her because I was familiar with the guys she was dealing with. I told her that she needed to calm down and show more respect for herself and to carry herself like a lady. She assured me that she would slow down, and she appreciated the counsel. Sister Bosh's husband was quickly drawn to me. He started referring to me as his "son" and I started calling him "godfather". I was the son he never had.

One of the elders from the congregation came to Sister Bosh's house to discuss with her and her "worldly" husband" that their daughter may have to be counseled with regards to her sexual behavior. If she didn't show any repentance; she would be read out in the congregation and put on public reprove. Sister Bosh and her husband got upset! They had been assured by the Elder that public reprove wasn't going to happen for their daughter. However they were lied to. Despite the reassurance from the elders, they put the daughter on public reprove anyway. Sister Bosh's husband felt that he was lied to. When the same Elder tried to visit the family again, her husband ran the Elder off his property and told him never to return. Regardless, I started to study with Sister Bosh's husband. Sister Bosh thought if any one could get him converted I would be the one to do it. I started having Bible discussions with him on Sunday; my mother thought this was the best thing since sliced bread. The Bible discussions were not in a conventional Jehovah Witnesses format, however. Sister Bosh's husband would cook dinner and would have a bottle of Jamaican Bacardi rum for us to drink. Sister Bosh would leave us alone. We would start off our bible studies with the protocol prayer and then we would have dinner, usually a big juicy steak and several glasses of rum and coke. We would talk about Bible scriptures that he was interested in and my view on them. I confessed to him that my mother wants me to be a baptized Jehovah Witness more than I did. I really didn't have too much choice. But I didn't mind talking to him about the Bible, and I wasn't there to convert him; I was just there as a friend. He appreciated the time and the sincerity of my visits. We became very good friends. We continued to have Bible discussions, and I counted our meetings as field service time. His wife didn't like the idea of us becoming friends. She wanted her husband studying the Bible with someone more spiritual. She was really disturbed by her husband inviting me to his job and telling his co-workers that I was his son. My mother thought studying with Sister Bosh's husband was in the right direction, progressing me spiritually towards Jehovah, dedication and baptism. You could not have told me that it would be less than a year for me to be tossed in the pool for baptism.

It was New Years Eve. I was celebrating, partying and rapping the night away at a house party. 1988 was looking promising, despite not having a record deal. I was still rhyming in the streets, on the radio, and still using Jehovah's name in my rhymes. I believed a record deal wouldn't be far away. I was going to shows with Mikey D and his L.A. posse around this time, setting myself up to perform my demos with him whenever time was permitted. He was scheduled to perform in Stamford, Connecticut during the week, on a Thursday night. I told him I was going to be there however I still had to ask my mom. I asked my mother if I could go to the show, telling her there was a slight possibility I might perform. She told me I couldn't because Thursday was a meeting night. She warned me that if I decided to go I'd better pack my belongings and leave the home that Friday. I informed Mikey D I couldn't go, and of course no reason was given. He didn't know I was going to the Kingdom Hall and there wasn't any reason to tell him now. It pissed me off! My mother was putting her foot down too hard on me. It motivated me to start calling my mother's brothers to see if I could live with them. I called my Uncle Earl first, who lived in Hartford, Connecticut. I told him that I needed to get out the house because mom wasn't letting me do anything unless it was Kingdom Hall related. I asked him if I could stay at his place for a while and start all over there in Hartford. I stated to him I would look for an apartment and employment. I just needed to get out of the house. He was sorry to hear what I was going through but he didn't want to get involved. I called my other Uncle in Washington DC, and asked him the same thing. He too declined, not wanting to get involved. Everyone in the family was scared of my mother. She seemed to possess evil powers that no one wanted to deal with. As soon as you mentioned my mother's name, they knew it wasn't going to be anything nice and pleasant. As the spring of 1988 approached, my mother had Brother James (the Elder that seemed sincere in helping me when I was 18) go over the 180 questions with me. The 180 questions are a required series of questions that must be answered and memorized to show dedication to Jehovah when getting baptized. Just because I knew all the answers at the *Watchtower* meetings and Tuesday night book studies didn't mean I was ready for that type of commitment. Dedication to Jehovah and baptism wasn't something I was ready for or had intentions of doing. I begged my mother not to do this, saying that I wasn't ready for baptism. Brother James came over to visit me and asked sincerely, "Is this something you want? Are you ready to do this, because this is a serious matter?" I replied, "This is something my mother wants, not me." I hinted to Brother James that what my mother was forcing me, but I never used the word "force". He suggested that I wait before going over the 180 questions and put the matter in prayer with Jehovah. I told my mother that Brother James stated that I needed to study on my own before going over the 180 questions again; it would be a couple of months. I was trying to buy some time so someone could get me out of that situation. I was 20 years old and thinking about how-in-the-hell I would get out of it. I called everyone on my mother's side of the family and was rejected. I hadn't communicated with my father's people since my father died in 1974. However, there was my Uncle Francis in Richmond, Virginia. He and his wife were living in a small house. I mentioned I was trying to get out of my house. Like everyone else, my Uncle Francis and his wife didn't want to be involved. Then, one day, my mother pulled me into the living room and inquired, "How come Brother James isn't doing the 180 questions with you?" I quickly informed her, "Brother James suggested I study some more, take some time and wait until I'm ready to answer them." My mother stated, "You are ready now! You should know the answers to those questions by heart." She continued, "You need to contact Brother James and tell him you will be ready for those 180 questions in a couple of *WEEKS!* I want you to be baptized by September, at the next circuit assembly. I told my mother that I wasn't ready and did not want to get baptized yet. I said, "Jesus didn't get baptized until he was in his early thirties, so what's the rush with me?" My mother looked at me and said calmly, "There is a scripture in the book of Genesis that speaks about honoring your mother and your days on this earth will be longer. You not getting baptized wouldn't be honoring Jehovah or _me_. You are being disobedient! Your guardianship account that you were supposed to receive when you turned 18, will now be available this coming August, when you turn 21. If you haven't dedicated your life to Jehovah, and haven't been baptized by the end of the year, you will not be receiving your money! Again she repeated, "You will have to be in good spiritual standing with me and Jehovah."

My mother handed me a document that she typed up stating the conditions for me to remain in the house, though the house was in my name. The document stated that in order to remain in the house I had to continue attending the Hall and all the meetings. I had to continue going out to field service and conducting bible studies. I had to dedicated my life to Jehovah and get baptized at the next circuit assembly. I also had to continue giving bible talks and continue growing spiritually. I would also have to remain in good standing with her and with the organization. If not, I would put my guardianship account money in jeopardy. If I couldn't abide by these stipulations, then I would have to leave the home immediately and that day. I had nowhere to go and wasn't making any real money to be out on my own yet, especially in New York City. There wasn't an apartment complex where you could walk in and put down a month or two months of rent. The waiting list for public housing was (and still is) 6 to 10 years. I just didn't have any time, and I didn't want my mother to mess up what was left of my guardianship account. I was livid that she had gotten to a point where she didn't care what I wanted. I begged her to stop acting like this and stop forcing me to do something I wasn't ready to do. My mother stated that I had to sign the document and she would sign it as well and she will have the block association president to notarize the document. I stated I hadn't dedicated my life to Jehovah and didn't have a clue on where to start. My mother told me to go upstairs and pray to Jehovah. She said for me to be creative in my dedication to Jehovah. I pleaded, "But mom, that's something that's serious. I don't know where to begin." She stated, "Dedicating your life to Jehovah is serious and so is being obedient! Go upstairs and make your dedication." I yelled back, "Suppose I tell the Elders about what you're doing to me, what you're forcing me to do?" She had a dead look on her face and politely said, "Let me tell you something right now, sweetie. If you decide to tell the Elders or anybody on me, YOU WILL REGRET IT AND IT WOULDN'T BE IN YOUR BEST INTEREST FOR YOU TO DO SO"! The statement felt like a knockout punch. I felt hopeless and empty and just out for the count. I really didn't know what to say or do. It felt like my mother had paid off everyone I had ever known in life. It was like everyone was in on it, and my mother had told everybody not to help me, and to let me suffer. If I told the Elders what my mother was doing, and showed them the document, maybe I'd have a fighting chance. I had to think about it first. Once I mentioned it to the Elders, it wouldn't be any turning back. They would investigate and there would be someone getting disfellowshipped. It would be my word against hers. But I had a copy of the document. That was physical evidence to show I wasn't making this up. If I reported this to the Elders and my mother ended up getting disfellowshipped, it wouldn't be a pretty sight ... there would be heavy consequences for reporting her. I never heard a case of a child reporting wrongdoing on a parent or parents. I dam sure didn't want to be the first. Plus, my mother said I would regret it. To hear that from her was like hearing it from a mafia boss. I never knew what would really happen. I thought about all the negatives and positives and concluded that it was just messed up with any choice I made. I was in a no win situation. I figured that if I got baptized I could buy myself some more time to figure out what I could do to get myself out of this situation. My mother still had access to my money, and she knew all my personal information. She had my name on the house, so I couldn't go far. I told my mother I would make my dedication to Jehovah and be ready for baptism at the next Circuit Assembly. My mother was delighted. I went upstairs to my room and closed the door. I made up some stupid dedication which made no sense and wasn't heartfelt at all. I don't even remember what I said but I made it sound good, at least to my ears. I came downstairs 20 minutes later and told my mother, "I made my dedication to Jehovah and I hope he was listening." I was being sarcastic. I didn't care. I didn't know how to make a dedication and didn't care about praying. What was I going to pray about? I already felt like my mother and Jehovah had a secret pact to ruin my life. There were no prayers to help matters. When Brother James came to the house to test me again with the

180 questions for baptism, he stated I did better than before and declared that I was now qualified for baptism. I told Brother James that I did my dedication and he asked me how I was feeling. He wanted to know if I was ready for baptism. There was some hesitation in me. Brother James looked at me and then looked at my mom. I finally said, "Yeah, I'm ready." He knew something was wrong. As long as my mother was in the same room with me, I wasn't going to give him any indication that my mother was making me get baptized. I think he sensed my mother was forcing me and deep down couldn't do anything about it. I wasn't ratting on my mother and my mother was in full control. Brother James could clearly see that. Until I spoke up, there wasn't much he could do or say. Regardless, the next circuit assembly wasn't until September 4, 1988 at the Assembly Hall in Jersey City, New Jersey. It was going to be a long summer. It was a summer that I would spend aggressively looking for a way out of this difficult situation that would ultimately change my life forever. Was I prepared to go up against the forces of deception and fear that my mother presented? Was I ready to expose her to the organization? Was I going to get baptized even when I knew I was knowingly being forced to? Afterwards, there would be the risk of me being exposed, living a double life. The idea of being disfellowshipped would be lurking right around the corner and staring me in the face every single day.

CHAPTER THIRTEEN: ITS 1988: DO YOU KNOW *WHO* BROTHER CHAMBERLAYNE IS?

The summer of 1988 arrived along with my 21st birthday. It was August 2nd and all I could remember was having fun celebrating hard, drinking twice as hard, and having sex harder than ever. I was just trying to remain positive and sane due to the circumstances. With the 180 questions answered to Brother James's satisfaction, I was now a candidate for baptism for the upcoming circuit assembly on September 4th, 1988. I tried to get in contact with my homeboy Tim who used to attend the Kingdom Hall but there was no success. I knew he was no longer living at home and I wasn't quite sure where he was. My 21st birthday came and went and my mother didn't mention anything about my guardianship account money. I thought about all the problems she put me through, especially forcing me to get baptized. I kept thinking that if I had my money, I wouldn't be going through this. I'd be sitting pretty somewhere far away from her. I confronted her again about my money and she said there wasn't any money left. All my money was gone; I was lied to again. I felt my mother had destroyed my life and I was her puppet. Now I was becoming a Jehovah Witness to become the organizations puppet. She told me the house was clear of any mortgages and in my name. She assured me that I always would have somewhere to live. Ironically, the same house with my name on the mortgage was also the same house I was trying to get out of and far away from her. I exhausted all possibilities for getting out of the house and trying to get out of being baptized. I had to face the reality that I would be a dedicated Jehovah's Witness and I would be called, "Brother Chamberlayne". My next move was to find the original document my mother made me sign. I found it in my mother's bedroom. The part about my guardianship account being in jeopardy had been covered up with whiteout.

She tricked me again into thinking there was something left of my money when in reality, she had stolen it and used it all up. I took the document anyway and made copies to show my friends. They couldn't believe it but they did understand what my mother was capable of. It's easy to say now, what I should have done, but back then, my mother put fear into me, mafia type of fear. My mother was banking on the fear that she instilled into me since I was 6 years old and the control she had on me. She was hoping fear would keep me from finding out what she did with my money. I could only count on one or two of my homeboys and a home-girl I just met a couple of months before the summer for help. My home-girl in Long Island was cool and wished that we could have gotten a place together. It just wasn't enough time as my countdown to baptism was ticking away day-by-day. No Elders or Brothers talked to me about how it was going to be. No one told me about any of their own personal experiences on when they had gotten baptized. I had no male figures in my life and never looked up to any Brother in the Kingdom Hall. Maybe the Brothers thought my mother was raising me well enough and I didn't need a man in my life to give advice or show me love. I didn't have a clue how to be a "Brother". The only love I had gotten from the Brothers was when they were trying to put me on public reprove or checking on my whereabouts, being Kingdom Hall detectives. I felt depressed and stressed out as my so-called big day approached and it showed all over my face. My facial skin was getting oily, and I started getting the worse case of acne and had to see a dermatologist. The doctor said that I needed to change my diet and that I had a lot of stress in me from worrying. She prescribed some vitamins and other pills, and my face cleared up within weeks. My stress level went down some as well. However, one Thursday night meeting proved fatal. I wasn't well and wanted to stay home. Despite telling my mother how I was feeling, she told me that I had to go to the meeting anyway. During the meeting at the Kingdom Hall, my stomach started bubbling but I thought it would get better but instead it got worse. The last Kingdom song was sung for the meeting and we were preparing to bow our heads to conclude the meeting with a prayer. After a few seconds into the prayer, I tried to whisk away so I could go to the bathroom. I was feeling extremely nausea by now. As I tried to step away, my mother grabbed my arm and motioned to me not to leave yet. It was her mistake. I threw up on myself and on the person in front of me. My mother was mad as hell, but she couldn't be too mad, after all, she stopped me from going to the bathroom thinking I was joking. I was still nervous, coupled with the pills I was taking. I laughed about it later when I got home and I started telling my mother maybe it was a sign not to get baptized from Jehovah. She just looked at me and walked away without any response. The last week before the Labor Day weekend was approaching and I had to meet up with an Elder and the other candidates who were getting baptized. We discussed our baptism and where we all had to meet and what we had to wear during and after the baptism. I found out there were eight others getting baptized from my congregation, including my homeboy Kendu. We were all nervous. I can honestly say that out of the eight individuals that were present to get baptized, three of us were going to have problems remaining faithful, and that included me. All eight of us were going to be taking this big step in our lives and I'm sure I wasn't the only one that was unhappy however there were little or no options. There were no baptism and dedication classes for us to attend and no discussions of what is expected when you get baptized. There was no buddy system to contact or to connect with. The organization didn't make this a joyous and wonderful event. I thought I would at least hear about some experiences from people who had gotten baptized and what that day meant to them. I was expecting to hear a lot more from the Brothers then what they were telling us. It was like the Elders said, "Your baptism is this Saturday, please make sure you are by the pool area 30 minutes before intermission. You should bring a bathing suit or swimming trunks and prepare to dive into the pool and submerge. Jump out and dry off. Congratulations, you are now Brothers and Sisters and representatives of Jehovah God. Stay focused and obedient. Please rat and report any wrongdoing. Watch your association. We all will be living on a paradise earth as promised; those that want to go further spiritually can go to heaven and be part of the 144,000 to help Jesus Christ rule. We will watch over the flock, so keep your eyes on the prize, sit back, don't worry, enjoy the ride and of course all of this in Jesus name, Amen. Thank you for coming and good night." And here I thought we were getting a certificate of baptism, but I guess not. When you get baptized in the organization, you don't get a certificate however it is recorded on your publisher's card.

My Baptism was September 4, 1988 and it started out as a warm Saturday morning. We had to be at the Circuit Assembly in Jersey City, New Jersey around 9:30 AM. This is a special day for many Jehovah's Witnesses because this day is considered your anniversary or your new spiritual birthday. I had my suit and a pair of swimming trunks and a white tee shirt. My mother was asking me several times about having a camera; I couldn't care less about preserving this memory. This was my mother's special day, not mine. My mother and I arrived at the Circuit Assembly and were told by an Elder that I had to be by the front of the stage 30 minutes before the intermission. When it was time, I went downstairs and sat near the stage. There was the pool and I saw our residing Elder from our congregation, Brother Farris. He shook my hand and I saw some other baptized Brothers from our congregation standing near by. My mother came down and took pictures along with some other Witnesses. When it was my time to get into the pool and be submerged, I already had my clothes and towel at the ready. I was summoned to get into the pool with a guiding Brother. I was motioned to move towards another Brother in the middle of pool. I did as instructed and he held my back and submerged me completely under, quickly bringing me back up. The friends were on the side clapping and taking pictures; my mother was among them, one of the loudest clappers. I'm glad she was happy about it all because I wasn't. I was helped out the pool and was instructed to dry off and put my clothes back on. As I walked back towards the restroom to put my suit on, I now realized that I just took the most important step in my life. It hit me when I looked in the mirror later in the restroom. I burst out laughing, looking at my reflection. *What did I just do?* I was laughing because deep down inside, I felt like a person that just got away with murder. I had this look of disgust and shame like I fooled them ... but I was only fooling myself. Not only was I now Brother Chamberlayne the hypocrite, but how long would it be before I'd be heading to see a disfellowshipped committee.

This was something my mother wanted, not me. I slapped her with that statement even when she congratulated me for doing such a noble deed as being baptized. To her, I was on the right path ... at least taking the right steps. Then it hit me! Why should I feel ashamed for doing what my mother wanted and not what I wanted? Jehovah already knew I didn't do this for myself, and He knows how I really felt. Wouldn't He know I was deceived and tricked and forced to do something I knew I wasn't ready for. After I thought about it in that way, I no longer felt guilty or ashamed. I was going to continue doing what I was already doing, regardless. I didn't care if I was called *"Brother Chamberlayne"* or not. When you get baptized, you are recognized as a Brother and a baptized Jehovah Witness, ready to fulfill certain obligations. One obligation is to lead the congregation in prayer no matter which meeting it is. My time of doing that would be coming in a matter of weeks thanks to Brother James. I was also put on the roster for holding the microphone for anyone that wanted to make a comment during the *Watchtower* meetings or the Thursday night meetings. I would be on the schedule to give bible talks and had to continue going out to field Ministry. When I was baptized on September 4, 1988, I was forgiven for all my past sins and shortcomings, everything I did up to that day. Every sex act, crime and wrongdoing I did before then was washed away. I was forgiven and received a new slate on September 4, 1988. All I had to do was stay out of trouble, commit no sins or wrongdoing, and report who was doing wrong. If I was doing wrong I had to make sure I didn't get caught, and if I was, I had to deny it all. I continued putting up a front with my everyday life and did my Kingdom Hall duties and obligations. Either way I would be guaranteed a spot to live forever on this paradise earth. I was ready to fool everybody that I was down with Jehovah. All that sounded good until reality set in just two days after I had gotten baptized.

It was Monday night, September 6, 1988; I was driving my car to Adelphi University to hang out at the radio station. I was still part of that hip-hop life, despite not having been there in weeks. The new radio DJ host was a college intern named "Wild Man Steve" and I came up there to show him some love and make a couple dedications. I needed some new girls' phone numbers. I stayed there till 12:30 in the morning but decided to leave early since I had to work in the morning. I figured I would be home by 1:00 AM. My friend Joe gave me some red headlight covers to put over my high beam lights, which I never used until that night. With my regular headlights already on, I didn't think it would be a problem to have my high beams on even though they were red and not white. I was driving down Hempstead Turnpike in Nassau County, where the police departments and officers are known to racial profile worse than NYPD, around 12:45 AM. I was driving my gray 1979 Cadillac Seville. My car wasn't in my name and my license was suspended. I passed a Nassau County cop car doing regular speed, but when he saw my high beam lights reflecting red, he immediately made a u-turn and came behind me, flashing his lights. At first I didn't get what the fuss was about. I was driving the speed limit and he didn't have psychic powers to know the conditions of my license. He followed me all the way down Hempstead Turnpike. I figured he would turn around when I reached the NYC County border by Belmont Race Track because he would be out of his jurisdiction. He couldn't cross over into Queens. I didn't know then that a police officer could go out of their jurisdiction if they are already in a pursuit. I crossed over into Queens and this Nassau County police officer was still flashing me to stop. I thought he wanted to do bodily harm to me because I wasn't cooperating. I panicked and drove faster! He decided that he would make me stop by getting in front of me and slowing his patrol car into mine causing a crash. This only scared me more; it looked like he wanted me dead! The last thing on my mind was pulling over somewhere that wasn't well lit or empty, without witnesses, just in case the officer decided to assault me. I decided to go all the way home no matter how many police officers had joined the chase and no matter how many traffic infractions I occurred. I was determined to get home to be around people just in case this cop decided to gun me down or rough me up. I drove down Jamaica Avenue until I reached some streets over by Jamaica Park by 203rd street. I then cruised towards 104th and 109th Avenues, continued across Hollis Avenue and down 109th Avenue. I turned onto Farmers Blvd, made a left and passed a crew of people standing on the street. I heard them cheering me on and laughing wondering what the hell I just did. I took Farmers Blvd to 113th Avenue and turned left, stopping at my mother's girlfriend house around the corner from where we lived. I jumped out and rang the doorbell quickly. My mother's girlfriend was hysterical. The Nassau County Cop pulled up right beside me, jumped out his patrol car and pulled out his weapon and demanded me to stand still. If I moved he said he would blow my head off. The officer was pretty shaken up and nervous. I wasn't sure if he was going to shoot or not. I later found out he was a rookie officer and I was his first high speed pursuit. He was very inexperienced and could have killed me. My mother wouldn't have been too pleased to see the headlines on the front cover of the New York Daily News: *RECENT BAPTIZED JEHOVAH WITNESS BOY SHOT DEAD BY POLICE!* I wonder if the Witnesses would have made some big media frenzy, holding press conferences and questioning the authorities, fighting for me like Revered Al Sharpton. It probably would have been a "no comment" statement from the society, swept under the rug and forgotten. As it turns out, the officer just wanted to tell me to turn off my high beam lights and that was it. The chase was finally over around 1:35 in the morning. I ended up going through 3 red lights, 4 stop signs, going up a one way street with speed exceeding over 90 mph, and damaging an officer's car, failure to pull over, illegal head light covers, a single count of 2nd degree reckless endangerment that involved two NYC police cars, 1 Nassau County police car, a fire trunk, and a NYC undercover car and hundreds of people outside watching in an excitement. Here I was a newly baptized Jehovah's Witness and already having the police pursue me in a high-speed car chase. I expected a call from the Elders on Tuesday and to be disfellowshipped by the end of the week. But I never received a call from the Elders because my mother didn't rat me out and neither did her two girlfriends that were Witnesses. I guess the Kingdom Hall watchdogs weren't out that night. Once again, my mother's questionable loving kindness was displayed and protected me from the Elders. The big payback was coming and it would be more than ten-fold in a matter of months.

CHAPTER FOURTEEN: KEEP YOUR EYES ON THE PRIZE

Everyone has eyes on some prize. Mine was getting out of my mother's house and finally looking forward to never attending the Kingdom Hall again. I stayed focus, concentrating on my prize of being free from all that I went through. When I heard the voice of my homeboy Tim, I knew I'd be getting my prize of freedom any day now.

I finally got a call from Tim late September '88. He was calling from Virginia Beach, and he had heard about me getting baptized. He already knew who was behind that move. I told him the whole story that I had been trying to locate him for a while. He told me he moved to VA Beach; he was living okay and asked was I okay. Of course I told him, *"HELL NO!"* I explained that my mother had me in a bad situation. I told him I needed a way out and how dead wrong my mother was on this Jehovah stuff. I asked Tim if he could help a brother out. He asked me would I want to come to Virginia and stay at his townhouse. Before he even finished the sentence, I shouted "WHEN?"

I told him I'd rent a car and come down to visit to check it out and make sure I liked it. But to me, it was already a done deal; it was just a matter of when. I was working at Cunard Cruise line on 5th Avenue and wasn't making any real money to be living on my own in New York, but maybe in Virginia … I could do a little something there. I was so excited about leaving home and not going to the Kingdom Hall any more. I could taste it. I had to plan this right. Nothing could backfire. I was looking into renting a car for a weekend to move for good at the beginning of the next year. I told my homeboy KB about my plans and asked if he could help me drive. He was cool with it and I proceeded to get things popping. I wished all of this could've happened before I was baptized but it was better late than never. I was still recognized as a Jehovah Witness and I had a publisher's activity tracking to deal with before I went anywhere. I told my friend Keith that I was leaving New York and going to Virginia Beach to live. I told him I had to get out of my house because I was tired of "fronting". The longer I stayed, the worse my relationship would get with my mother. My friend Keith told me to be careful and if I had any problems in Virginia to just come back. He said he would come up with another plan and put something into action if needed. I wasn't trying to get approval but I needed to let certain people know what I was doing. I asked Tim about the climate in VA Beach and he said I would have to come down and check it out because it may not be to my liking. I was willing to do whatever it took to leave my present situation. As I started getting my plan into action, I had to think about when I was going to tell my mother about leaving New York to go VA Beach. I didn't want to tell her too soon and have her sabotage my plan.

Back at the Kingdom Hall, I was "Brother Chamberlayne" and when you are baptized, you are considered an ordained minister in the organization and have some obligations to fulfill like all baptized brothers. A month after I was baptized, Brother James, who went over the 180 questions with me, wanted me to conclude the Thursday night meeting with prayer over the congregation. I knew I had to do it sooner or later but I preferred later. As I got up out of my seat, I walked slowly to the stage thinking about what the hell I was going to say. I had been going to the Hall all these years and listened to thousands of brothers pray before, but I never had to pray. I damn sure didn't want to start now. The first thing that came to mind was to acknowledge Jehovah and His son Jesus Christ. When I reached the stage, another Brother adjusted the microphone stand for my height and I looked out into the congregation and said, "Let's bow our heads." Then I said something similar to what I heard over the years in the prayers of others. I concluded by saying "I say this prayer in Jesus' name, Amen." I walked off stage and back to my seat. I received nods of approval and of course my mother saying, "You sure know what to say when you're under pressure, huh?" I said, "Timing is everything, right?" She replied, "It sure is, sweetie," and when she said that, I laughed to myself on the inside. I was thinking, *"Just wait until January, because timing sure was everything."* Some sisters in the congregation approached me, giving me hugs and kisses on the cheek and saying, "Your mother has done such a beautiful job with you and Jehovah really has blessed you." I walked away thanking them and saying to myself, *"If only you knew the truth."*

The prayer I said over the congregation that Thursday night might've been pleasing and well received and some might have perceived me as going in the right direction spiritually. But, not all saw it that way. There are people ready to receive a Medal of Honor and praise for telling the Elders about a wrongdoing or a suspicion of a wrongdoing. There was an over zealous Brother that was younger than me in age but had been baptized longer. He saw me walking past his grandmother's house where he lived. He was going to work that morning and didn't have a clue where I was coming from. That Sunday afternoon meeting (our congregation meeting time had changed to the afternoon) I saw him after the meeting and I said, "What's up?" He replied with the same. He didn't mention to me that he saw me earlier that morning, however, Brother James came by where I was sitting at and asked, "Do you have a minute so I can ask you something?" I answered politely, "Sure. What's up?" He stated to me that a certain Brother in the congregation saw me early that morning around 5 AM walking the streets. I looked at Brother James and said, "Really? Why didn't this Brother speak? And if this Brother saw me at 5 AM in the morning, what was he doing up that early himself?" Brother James said, "I was told by the Brother that he was going to work." I came back at him and said, "Do you think perhaps, that I could've been coming home from work as well. Besides, the last time I checked, I was over 21 and older than the Brother that reported this to you. I already know who it is." Brother James said, "That could be the case," and gave me a funny look as he walked away. He never mentioned this incident to me again. There is always somebody ready to report something to the Elders. With me being baptized now, it was going to get worse. I would have to walk a straight line for the next three more months and hopefully my publisher's record could be sent to Virginia without any blemishes.

I called Tim down in VA Beach, telling him that I was coming down for the weekend to check things out. I informed him that I was bringing KB who was my 'worldly' childhood friend that lived on my block with me. I rented a car and left Friday night. I drove most of the way down to Virginia. I followed the directions to where Tim was staying and found out it was an off-the-chain 2-bedroom apartment! It had waterbeds in each bedroom and a fireplace. I thought I had the wrong place. Tim couldn't be living here looking like it was a vacation resort. He said I could chill on the couch in the living room because his other homeboy James had the second bedroom. I didn't care if I had to sleep on the floor, that's how excited and happy I was leaving my house in New York. While I was there, I saw damn near half my neighborhood of Hollis, Queens as well. I saw a handful of other people like my friend Cal and Rodney and one of Rodney's cousins.

We all had a good time partying and drinking, going to the mall shopping and meeting new girls. The trip was too quick. When I got back to New York, I informed my mother that I'd be moving to Virginia Beach with Tim for good. My mother liked Tim because he used to go to the Kingdom Hall. She knew he was a sincere friend to me and she didn't object when I told her about Virginia Beach. However, she was concerned about the activities and the work we would be involved in. I told her I would be quitting the accounts payable job I had at Cunard Cruise LTD and would get another job in Virginia. She suggested that if I moved to Virginia in January, then she would consider moving back to the town where she was raised (Gretna, Virginia), 4 hours away from VA Beach. I said, "I thought you liked it here and hated Gretna, Virginia! How could you consider leaving all your Kingdom Hall friends?" Of course I was being sarcastic but I had to wonder why she suddenly wanted to move to Virginia, when I wanted to move to Virginia. I told her I was leaving in the next two months and I was taking all my belongings with me. I informed her that I wouldn't be going to the Kingdom Hall there in Virginia Beach. She wasn't too pleased to hear that but she couldn't do anything about it. She suggested to at least having my publisher's card go the congregation in Gretna, Virginia even though I wasn't going to be attending. She stated that the Queens' congregation would not have my publisher's record and that would eliminate the Elders from trying to find me because I would be in the Gretna congregation once they received confirmation I was 'attending' there. My mother said, "I know how sneaky and trifling the Elders are at our congregation, especially Brother Farris. He is so mad at you because you won't pay his precious daughter any attention. The Elders are mad because they always want to know my business and I don't tell them anything because my business doesn't pertain to them. Maybe leaving this congregation and moving to Virginia would be good for both of us." She was tired of dealing with some of "the friends" in our congregation, particularly the Elders. She started putting into works her own plans to relocate and buy another house in Gretna, Virginia. The last couple of weeks in New York, I applied for two credit cards and handed in my resignation to my job a month in advance. I told everyone I was moving to Virginia. The congregation had already started gossiping about me leaving, thinking I was going to Gretna, Virginia instead of Virginia Beach. My mother told me she would make sure my publisher's card was sent to the congregation in Gretna, Virginia even though I wouldn't be attending the Gretna congregation. She called some of "the friends" from Gretna, Virginia to give them a heads up that I would be down there sometime in January or February of next year. She even told them that she might follow suit later on in the year. My mother had it all planned, telling even the most curious Elders that I would be attending the Kingdom Hall in Gretna, Virginia. This would cover me; there would be no red flags raised about my spirituality since I just had gotten baptized some months ago.

My mother was actually trying to protect me from the Elders, the same elders that she was protecting herself from. But was she trying to protect herself by covering for me knowing I wasn't going to Gretna, Virginia? I guess she felt the need to protect the only one that could expose her to the Elders about what she forced me to do. I couldn't care less. I went along with her program. All I cared about was that I wouldn't be entering another Kingdom Hall again and my Jehovah's Witness days would be coming to a glorious end. After 14 years of being forced to go and make comments at the meetings, having water thrown on me and much more, I was going to be free. They could've been told I was going to visit the North Pole by railroad; I didn't care. However, there was still an issue of me being baptized. That issue would have the Elders in the congregation keeping tabs on me if I decided to pop back up somewhere down the road. The Elders in the congregation were reluctant about sending my publisher's card to the congregation in Gretna. They wanted confirmation that I was there or to received notice that I was coming to the Gretna congregation. My mother either sent a letter or called the Elders in Gretna, Virginia. She stated that I would be attending their congregation in the coming weeks and to please request my publisher's record. I told the Elders in Queens I was going to Virginia (I never said where) and to send my publisher's card to the congregation in Gretna. My mother wanted to at least make sure my publisher's record was gone before I left. My last week attending the Kingdom Hall gave me the weirdest feeling because I had been going to this congregation since 1974 and everyone here watched me grow up into manhood. There were people here that had known me for over have my life. It was hard to believe that after 14 years, I was getting sentimental about leaving. This was like my second home and my spiritual comfort zone.

I didn't know anything else but going to the Kingdom Hall. I would always be connected to this congregation no matter how my life turned out. I gave my last bible talk on Thursday night. As I said my last words, I looked at the congregation and thought to myself, *"It's time to enjoy my second life."* I had been dreaming about Virginia and started suddenly feeling like a fish out of the water. I asked myself if Jehovah would continue to bless me and to protect and shield me from the worldly temptations. I was leaving to be part of the world, out on my own without Jehovah's protection and guidance and there was no turning back. I shook everyone's hand and hugged all the sisters in the congregation knowing in my heart, this would be the last time I would be in this Kingdom Hall. I walked out of Kingdom Hall reminiscing about how I used to bust rhymes about the Kingdom Hall on the street corner of Hollis Avenue and 201st street just across the street. I gave my last look at the sign on the brown building, "The Kingdom Hall of Jehovah's Witness" and I walked away jumping up and down and smiling. It was one of the best feelings I ever had.

CHAPTER FIFTEEN: THE ELDERS ARE CALLING FOR A COMMITTEE

1989. I was living life in Virginia Beach the way I was suppose to when I was in New York. I was drinking, partying and having sex with every girl I came across, trading them off for my friends when I was finished with them when I was done. I was living my life without the scrutiny of the Elders with no Jehovah's Witness in sight to report me. The association that I once shared with "the friends" was a thing of the past. I didn't have a guilty conscious and didn't think I should. I had been living like this before I was baptized. Getting baptized meant nothing to me because it wasn't heartfelt; it was done by force, not by choice. I was still the horny sinner that was committing fornication and doing every vile sexual act that was conceived. This was the first time in my adult life I had freedom and I didn't know how to act. I was waking up late Sunday mornings without my mother forcing me to get out of the bed or throwing cold water on me, and it felt great. There where no more meetings, no more field service, no more memorials, no more district and circuit assemblies, no more bible studies, no more prayers, no more bible talks, no more Watchtowers and Awake magazines, no more Jehovah Witnesses reporting to my mother on my whereabouts, no more anything Kingdom Hall related.

While in New York, my mother was preparing to buy another house in her hometown of Gretna, Virginia. She found one not far from where my grandparents were living. The price of the house was a steal; my mother bought it. The house that I was raised in was still in my name and free and clear of any bank mortgages. Any home equity loans that my mother needed had to go through me, or at least that's what I thought. I also thought that this was the only mortgage that would be against the house. My mother called me while I was settling in Virginia Beach and told me to come back to New York for a week so I could get an equity loan against the house for her. She already had the paper work completed; I just had to show all my credentials and proof of employment (which I didn't have at that time). My mother used one of my pay stubs from my old job I just quit a month ago and surprisingly, the loan processor accepted the pay stub and the loan was approved. This equity loan was for $54,000 and she needed around $70,000 to do the deal. To my surprise, my mother had already had taken out two different mortgages against the house. This was done without my knowledge or signatures. My mother had all the money she needed to buy the house in Gretna, Virginia in cash. To this day, I still don't know how she was able to obtain two equity loans without my signatures, unless she forged them. My mother bought the house in Gretna, Virginia in cash with a certified check. She wanted to rent the house in New York to a Jehovah Witnesses couple from our old congregation. I suggested to my mother that renting out the house to Jehovah Witnesses wouldn't be a great idea because they would cause problems for both of us. Plus, they were too damn nosey and liked to gossip and spread rumors. I suggested to my mother that she rent out the house to my childhood friend June. He would pay a certain amount of money on the mortgages, and if needed, I would come back up from Virginia and help. My mother didn't like my idea and went with having the Witnesses renting out the house. The husband, Brother Earl, was making excellent money and the couple would be able to afford the rent and upkeep.

After several months of trying to find a job and partying and getting into trouble, I was hesitate on leaving Virginia Beach and returning back to New York. I just couldn't find a job nowhere, however, there was something in me saying that I should try doing rap music again, however, I just needed a confirmation of what I was thinking. Well, someone did confirm what I was thinking and it was from someone I least expected. While listening to the radio, I heard the rap group Public Enemy on the air and the group was in town to do a show in Hampton, Virginia. I called the radio station and spoke to Chuck D and told him I was now living in Virginia Beach. He stated to me what hotel they were staying at and come check him. I arrived at the hotel that they were staying at and saw Chuck D and some other members of the group I knew. We talked about what was going on with the group and had the opportunity to listen to some new music they did in the studio and a "live freestyle" tape that the group did on a radio station in the country of Japan. While listening to the tape, I started to freestyle rapping along with the music that the group was rapping to on the tape. Group member "Flavor Flav" heard me rapping and said, "Yo Geechie, you nice G". I said, "You think so Flavor"? He said, "Yeah G, you should go back to New York and get a deal G." When I heard him say that, going back to New York didn't sound so far fetched. The more I thought about what he said, the more I was convinced that being in Virginia Beach wasn't the place for me. Relocating to Virginia Beach served its purpose but going back to New York to live with my mother wasn't something I was going to do either. It was time to think of a game plan just like my man Keith used to say. Then it hit me just that quickly, I needed to call Keith and tell him what I wanted to do and maybe come up with a solution. I called Keith and he said to just get back to New York the fastest and the best way you can and we will figure something out. When I arrived in New York, I stayed with my friend Keith in the Lower East side for a while to figure out where can I permanently stay at since going back to live with my mother wasn't an option. I stayed with him for a couple of months and then landed right back in Hollis, Queens staying right around the corner from where I grew up at, staying at my mother's best friend's home. I stayed around the corner for several months until my mother moved to Virginia permanently. Once my mother relocated to Virginia for good, she wanted me to come back to the house, watch the tenants, and help on the upkeep of the house and stay in the basement. I didn't think it was a bad idea then to stay rent-free at my old house and have the basement to myself. I came back to the house and I figured I'd stay in the basement. The basement had its own phone line and the Jehovah Witness tenants living upstairs wouldn't bother me. Just as I thought, problems began occurring for my mother, and I was caught right in the middle. This, of course, created problems for me. After several months, the couple had the nerve to conduct a Tuesday night book study without telling my mother. The couple had a 'worldly' nephew staying with them since they first moved in the house. They wanted their nephew out of the house because they suspected he was into criminal activity and may cause problems. The nephew didn't move out of the house. Instead, he bounced back and forth from the basement (when I wasn't there) to staying upstairs, hiding when they weren't home. I eventually caught him and we exchanged words and fists in the driveway. I had wondered for weeks, how my items and my loose change would just disappear when I wasn't home. Then the Jehovah's Witness couple that was living in the house started rumors about me having orgies in the basement, smoking cigarettes and doing crack cocaine. They said that drug dealing was going on, that I wasn't going to the meetings, and that I wasn't attending the book study on Tuesday evening right upstairs in my own house. I wasn't attending the meetings, but none of the other activities were going on; however, the damage was already done. The only people from my old congregation that knew I was back in my old area of Hollis, Queens were my mother's best friends from around the corner. When I appeared back at my house, word quickly got out that I had returned. My mother's friends heard these rumors about me all the way in Virginia. My mother called the Jehovah's Witness couple and asked them to mind their own damn business and leave my affairs alone. She demanded they stop spreading "untruths" about me to other Witnesses. The coupled claimed they weren't the ones spreading "untruths" about me. But, the rumors stopped. My mother thought everything was fine, but it wasn't. She had to call the couple again about another situation regarding me. This time my mother let the wife have it over the phone. She decided that the couple had to leave; she started plotting ways to make the couple leave on their own. She wanted this to be done in a tactful manner. She had to get them out the house and make sure it was done without any legal issues or lawsuit, even though Jehovah's Witnesses are not supposed to sue each other. This also had to be done without the attention of the Elders. My mother came up from New York on a weekday and spoke to a retired Con Edison electrician about a wiring issue that was occurring behind the walls of the house. The scenario was such that it wasn't safe for occupants living at the house because the electrical current had to be shut off and investigated by inspectors before allowing anyone back inside myself. The couple said at first that they were going to stay there and honor the lease agreement. My mother said, "Fine, as long as you are aware that the electricity will be off and there will be no heat, hot water, stove and no lights." They were pretty upset. After a week of living in the house without electricity, they packed up all their belongings and moved. I left the house as well to act like I was moving too, but after they left; I came back home and just turned on the electrical breaker for the basement. But my mother had to get another tenant into the house quick; she didn't want to lose more than 2 months rent, despite not paying a dime on the mortgages. I had spoken to my mother briefly over the phone and she asked, "Sweetie, had you had anyone over to the house or in the house?" I told her no. Because of the events that had just taken place, I didn't want anyone around. With the Jehovah Witness couple already having a bad taste in their mouths, they started running their mouths about what my mother had done to them. Now I had to deal with rumors about my mother coupled with rumors about me. I wanted to remain low-key for a couple of weeks. If anyone came around, I wouldn't answer the door. I knew for a fact the Elders would question my return to New York and why I was not attending any meetings. They would also want my mother's contact information. I was going to avoid giving out her number unless she permitted me to do so. I would instead get their number and pass it back to my mother. A couple of days had passed and the Jehovah's Witness couple was gone for good. I was still worried that the couple might send someone to pass through the block just to see if the lights were on. My mother instructed me to leave the upstairs lights off completely; however, the electrical breakers for the kitchen stove and the hot water heater could be turned on. She also instructed me not to leave the TV on at night because the TV light could be seen from outdoors. As unusual, during the week, I would be in the basement eating or watching TV, talking on the phone trying to get a girl to come over for some company and sex and getting my clothes ironed out for work the next day. I received a phone call from a woman that used to attend the Kingdom Hall. It had been years since I'd heard from her and we were talking up a storm. I thought she was looking for my mother to pass some information for her relatives. She and her sister were some wild girls back in the days. While we on the phone, we decided to talk about those days. She was talking to me about the stuff she had done in her past and making me feel at ease by using some curse words and slang, giving me the impression that she wasn't spiritual at all and not a baptized Jehovah's Witness Sister. I talked about my rapping and things that I had done before I was baptized. It was then that the subject about girls came up; she wanted to discuss some of my sexual encounters. I didn't feel comfortable discussing *all* my sexual encounters but what I didn't catch was that she was only interested in hearing about any sexual encounters ***after*** I was baptized. She said playfully, "Go ahead and tell me about your stories," like it turned her on. I only thought this could lead to sex. I started thinking about all my sexual encounters that I had after I had been baptized, picking and choosing stories like I was putting my hand into a grab bag. I figured her being a woman she might not want to hear about anything too graphic and sexual. I told her about a simple encounter that I had with this girl in Virginia Beach and if that aroused her interest and depending on her response, then, I would discuss another encounter. I told her that the sexual encounter I had with this girl was a one-time encounter and we both used protection and I never saw her again. Her response was like, "Okay that was nice but what about some details." She started acting like an undercover cop with her responses and I received a bad vibe that she wasn't the sex freak I thought she still was. I became reluctant to talk anymore about sex. I said, "Yeah, you know, shit happens." and quickly changed the subject. It seemed after I told her about that one sexual encounter, that she had heard enough about my fornicating act. She made a quick excuse to get off the phone. I didn't feel well about this conversation after all. I told her to keep in touch and she told me to enjoy the rest of the evening and hung up. Later on that evening, I received another phone call. These were the days before caller ID, so I let the phone ring several times thinking it was girl calling to hookup for the night. I picked up the phone and to my surprise, it was Brother Badstone on the line. I was thinking to myself it was too much of a coincidence that he was calling. He had been trying for years to get dirt on me and have me reported for wrongdoing. He was calling to confirm about an earlier conversation I had that evening with some baptized Sister I said, "Sister who?" I didn't recall having a conversation with this so-called Sister but I did speak to my old associate. Brother Badstone said, "That woman you were speaking to earlier is a baptized Sister and she related to me how disturbed she was about some fornicating acts you were involved in. There are also other matters of some disturbing rumors that need to be addressed. We will have to discuss this matter further with a committee." I said, "Sure Brother Badstone. When and where can this be discussed?" He said, "I will get back to you on a time, date, and place." I said, "That's fine, just let me know." He apologized for calling so late and said, "I will be in touch. Have a good night." I said, "Thanks." and hung up. When I hung up the phone, I said to myself, "This was the best set up I ever heard of. The FBI couldn't pull off something like this, isn't this something?"

I paced back and forth in the basement that night kicking and punching the wall and hitting my chest for allowing myself to be stupid enough to talk about anything I did to someone I really didn't know. I said aloud again, "This chick played my ass and she was down with Jehovah all along!" I felt like calling the chick back in the late hours of the night and using every kind of profanity possible to her. I said, "Yeah, she got me real good."

After tossing and turning all night, unable to sleep, I was thinking, *Could this be a blessing in disguise?* After all, I wasn't attending any meetings and haven't been to a Kingdom Hall for almost a year now. I had been baptized since September of 1988 by force and not by choice. I was also enjoying my newfound freedom and wasn't up to fronting anymore. Come on! I was having sex before I was baptized and I was still having sex, nothing changed. So whom was I fooling?

The Elders were going to hold a committee. I had to know how to answer them and not get upset about the false rumors. I had to answer for the whereabouts of my mother and anything dealing with the house. I only wanted to talk about facts, not rumors and what kind of spiritual help needed. The fornication issue was something I could've denied. I could tell them I lied about it all just to impress a woman. She was trying to seduce my innocence. I'd tell them I was still a virgin. I mean, how would they know? It would've been my word against hers. The only advantage she had was that she was an active and faithful servant of Jehovah and she proved her loyalty to the organization by turning me in to the Elders. I on the other hand was the complete opposite. I hadn't been to a meeting in almost a year; I wasn't even attending the book study that was being held at my own house. I hadn't been in field service in a year and my mother was someone the Elders were looking for. I was screwed with the fornicating issue (no pun intended). Once I received that call from Brother Badstone, I knew the outcome of all of this would be another life altering event. However, I thought maybe it was time to put this all to closure and move on with my life. I didn't like the way in which I was confronted with this issue because it was an issue I tried to avoid for years. I begged my mother not to have me in this predicament but she wanted dedication and baptism. Since she was fine with me living a lie, then I guess she wasn't going to have any issues with me being disfellowshipped either. After all, my mother was the one that forced me into baptism. The Elders wasn't looking to read me a bunch of scriptures for nothing. They wanted my mother disfellowshipped and me! I dreaded the few options I had. My 1st option: **telling the elders about the document I had to sign and how my mother forced me to get baptized.** The 2nd option: **get disfellowshipped and never have to worry about this organization again.** The 3rd option: **deny everything and lie and continue fronting.** The 4th option: **getting disfellowshipped and then apply for reinstatement.** That was it. Whatever option I decided, that's what I was going to stick with. After that, I would move on.

CHAPTER SIXTEEN: DISFELLOWSHIPPED

I know this will be a touchy subject to discuss. This may probably be the most interesting chapter to read. I can visualize some baptized Jehovah's Witnesses reading and scanning through the book and reading only this chapter just to see how I got disfellowshipped. To some, this is the "good part" and the "juicy part" of the book. It wasn't something I was looking forward to writing, however, it's something that happened to me and will always be attached to me.

It was during the winter of 1989, going into the New Year. I was living back in Hollis, Queens, New York, at my house in the basement, working at an Investment firm in lower Manhattan. I also started attending the College of New Rochelle in Manhattan. Throughout this time I'd been having a tough time trying to get a hold on the financial mess my mother put me. I was making just enough money to live in the basement. I wasn't paying on any of the mortgages because I felt that my name on paper was already ruined, and my mother never paid on any of the mortgages with the money she received through the loans and from the rent she was getting from the Jehovah's Witness couple that used to live upstairs. I figured going back to school would keep my mind off my mother, the house, and the recent issues with the Elders. I called my mother in Virginia and told her what had happened with the Elders and their meeting with me. She was livid. She told me how stupid I was for getting mixed up in all this. She also claimed the Elders were doing this because they couldn't get to her directly; my mother was always getting around them. She claimed that the reason the Elders were doing this was to get back at her. She continued, "The Elders are probably trying to get your publisher's card returned to the Murdock Congregation from the congregation in Gretna as we speak." I said, "Yeah, I know." She did advise me to avoid meeting with the Elders and come to Gretna. If the congregation in Gretna, Virginia still had my publisher's card, the Elders in New York would have to contact the Elders in Gretna, Virginia about any of my wrongdoing. It would be better to go through the Elders in Gretna, Virginia than the Elders up in New York. As always, my mother was looking for a way for me to dodge them. She could run circles around them. The Elders wouldn't have a fighting chance, even if they had help. My mother would come out victorious. I expected these types of games when having worldly dealings, but not in a spiritual organization of Jehovah. Unfortunately, these games are played even in religion, and it's sad. My mother also mentioned, not to have the Elders calling her or trying to contact her about anything. I didn't tell my mother *exactly* what happened yet, not in detail. But she was pretty sure her name would come up in conversations with the Elders. She warned me again, *"DO NOT HAVE THOSE ELDERS FROM THE MURDOCK CONGREGATION CONTACTING ME ABOUT ANYTHING!"* I told my mother the Elders wouldn't be contacting her about anything. I assured her that whatever decision the Elders made would be based on the facts and not any rumors that involved her. For some reason my mother didn't have any faith in the Elders at the Murdock Congregation. They couldn't care less about what my wrongdoing was. She already knew what their decision was going to be. While my mother was scheming and searching for loopholes, I was anticipating getting this over with. Telling the Elders that what occurred in Virginia was a one time only fornication act with a girl. I wouldn't entertain anything concerning my mother. I received a call from Brother Badstone a couple of days later and was instructed to be present for a "judicial committee" that involved a meeting of three Elders from the congregation. The residing Elder or "Head Elder" picks the Elders. The three Elders, and the accused, meet and discuss the wrongdoing or the offense and then proceed to administer spiritual counsel and discipline. It's almost like a spiritual court. I was told that Brother Ivory and Brother James would be the other two Elders that would be joining the committee. We all were going to meet at Brother James' house. I told Brother Badstone that I wouldn't be able to meet with them during the week because I had to work. The weekend would be better. I was doing this just to annoy them. If I was going down, I wanted it to be on my terms. I got another call, this time from Brother James. He was calling to remind me of our meeting this coming weekend, to make sure I was on time at his house. I told him I could make it, that I wanted to start this process and hopefully receive some spiritual help. It was a cold, cloudy day. I arrived at Brother James's house and saw him and the other two Elders, Brother Ivory and Brother Badstone. To my amazement, I didn't see the young lady that reported me to the Elders. I asked Brother James, "Where is the young lady that reported me?" Brother Badstone said, "I took her statement Danny. She doesn't need to be present." I didn't think this was fair. The Elders said they were trying to prepare a welcoming atmosphere so I would feel comfortable. I knew they would be checking out my mannerisms and looking at my physical appearance. They hadn't seen me for over a year. They were checking to see how worldly I had become. The Elders asked how I was doing and I said, "Spiritually, I could be doing better. But I'm fine despite what I'm going through." The Elders said almost condescending like, "We understand that you are living in the basement of your house. We wanted to know why you were not attending the meetings". Before any conversation could continue, the Elders suggested that I get comfortable and relax. I guess having me being comfortable and relaxed, I was more willing to spill the beans on everything. They probably thought to themselves, "We finally are going to get the "Chamberlayne's! But before any anticipation of hearing words of guilt, we had start off this court session with a prayer to Jehovah. The Elders then asked about my financial welfare. They wanted to know how my mother was doing and if she was still in Virginia. I stated plainly that I wasn't there to take up valuable time discussing anything that wasn't spiritual. I did assure them that my mother was fine and still living in Virginia. The Elders stated that the contact information they had wasn't valid. They were unsuccessful in contacting my mother. These types of questions went on for 15 minutes before I asked the Elders if I was there to discuss my spirituality or my mother's whereabouts. The room got quite and the subject turned to the real reason why we were there. They agreed, reluctantly, that we should be discussing the fornicating incident in Virginia that was reported to them. I told them I met a girl in Virginia last year and we had consensual sex one time, and we both used protection. As I was telling them about the incident, their pens were hitting the pads taking notes. They then started with the questions. *How old was this woman?* I said, "She was younger than me." *Was she in "the truth" or a worldly woman?* I said, "A worldly woman." *What kind of protection was used?* I said, "Several boxes of condoms were used." Of course that statement made them pause and look at each other before continuing. *Were we dating or girlfriend/boyfriend?* I said, "It was a one night stand and it only happened that one time." *Is this woman still living in Virginia?* I said, "Yes." *Have you been involved with any other sex relations since that incident in Virginia?* I said, "No, I have not." *Have you had any sexual incidents or group sex in your basement?* I said, "No, there haven't been any orgies or group sex going on in my basement, despite what you heard." It was like they didn't believe me and wished that the rumors were true. They seem to enjoy my interrogation too much. I felt like the information was too private for discussion. Some of their questions didn't relate to my wrongdoing. It was like going to court without any representation. There were no lawyers, no defense team, no rebuttals, no character witnesses, not even the girl I was on the phone with that reported me. I probably should have lied about everything since I was already holding back information and being judged. I started getting upset and defensive because everything I did for over 16 years for the organization just didn't matter; all my good standing and baptism went right down the drain. All my field service time, Bible talks, and Bible studies I used to conduct. Attending the Kingdom Hall meetings (even when forced to) just wasn't enough, at least not for me anyway. I wondered if I were an Elder's son if I would have received any special treatment. That was all the questions that were asked at this first judicial meeting. Then the Elders started discussing some scriptures from the New World Translations Bible that pertained to fornication. The scriptures in the Bible were explained in great detail on how they applied to my wrongdoing. The scriptures were *Revelations 21:8, 1 Corinthians 6:9 and verse 18, 1 Corinthians 5:13, 1 Corinthians 6:15-20, 1 Corinthians 7:2, and Hebrews 13:4.* The scriptures talked about how much God despised fornication and that no fornicators would inherit God's kingdom and how fornicators and adulterous ones will be judged. The Elders continuously asked if I was repentant and sorry for my actions. I said, "Yes. What could I do to repair this wrongdoing? Scriptures do help some, but what else can I do?" The Elders asked, "Are you planning on attending the meetings?" I said, "No. I have to work." The Elders asked if I would be able to attend Sunday meetings. I said, "No. I can't at this time. My financial state is in shambles. Mentally, I wasn't ready to attend any meetings." I explained further, "I don't want to give the impression that I don't want any spiritual help because that's not the case. But, my mental and financial affairs are just as bad as my spiritual state and need to be attended to as well." I continued, "I don't want you and the other Elders to feel that I'm not repentant or have the wrong attitude about this. I told you the truth. I have dismissed the rumors about me, been accurate about the whereabouts of my mother, and a fornication act was a one time thing." They said they would take that statement into consideration. The Elders advised me to continue praying over all my matters and said we'd be able to wrap this up next week. They made some suggestions about reading scriptures and then we concluded the first judicial meeting with a prayer. I was informed that we would be meeting again next weekend, same time and place. I now was optimistic about the whole judicial process. I wondered if I was doing the right thing. I wasn't so sure, however. I knew I wasn't living right. I needed to meet with someone about a wrongdoing, but maybe the timing wasn't right. Maybe meeting with these Elders wasn't such a good idea. With the false rumors about me going around, the Elders looking for my mother and the recent situation of the Jehovah's Witness couple, I couldn't see where or how the outcome of this would be fair. My mother might've been right in regards to talking with these Elders. But if she had just listened to me about having those Jehovah's Witnesses from our old congregation in the house, I wouldn't have gone through any of this mess. The week turned into days, the days into hours, and the hours into minutes. Finally the day I dreaded arrived. I took that nine-block walk slowly. The weather was just like it was on the previous weekend meeting. It was cold and windy and I was catching a bad cold. I saw the Elders' cars parked outside Brother James' home. I walked up the steps and rang the bell wishing no one answered. Brother James greeted me at saying, "Oh, yes, Brother Chamberlayne." How are you doing this cold afternoon?" I answered, "It could be a lot better, Brother James." I sat down where the Elders were already sitting on the couch.

They asked that we start off our judicial meeting with a prayer to Jehovah and one of the Elders proceeded in prayer. I was then served hot tea and Brother Ivory told me to open up my Bible to read the book of Acts 26:20. The scripture talks about producing works that befit repentance, which basically meant I failed to show any works that I was genuinely repentant. I hadn't been attending meetings or showcased a humbling attitude. The next scripture read was Matthew 18:15-17. It spoke about reporting a Brother or a Sister of wrongdoing to the Elders and if that individual refuses to hear even them, then that individual should be treated like a tax collector. The third scripture was James 5:16. This scripture said that it is okay to report the trespasses of others. The fourth scripture that was read was Jude Chapter 1 verse 21-23, which says the elders have the spiritual qualifications to restore or reprove and to have compassion for some but save others with fear. I was hearing all of this and knew it wouldn't be too much longer before the evitable. The fifth scripture was 2 Timothy 3:16 and 17. That scripture says in brief that all scriptures are from GOD and they are to be used for doctrine, for reproof, for correction, for instruction and for righteousness. The sixth scripture was 2 Timothy 4:1 and 2. This was about preaching the word and to convince rebuke, exhort with all longsuffering and teaching. The seventh scripture was 1 Timothy 5:17-20. This said the ruling Elders would be counted worthy of double honor, especially those who labor in the word and doctrine; verse 20 said those sinning need to rebuke in the presence of all, which the rest also may fear. I kept saying to myself, *the guilty verdict would be said any minute now. I don't know why they keep teasing me.* The eighth scripture read was 1 Corinthians 5:11-13, talking about not keeping company with anyone named a brother who is a fornicator and not even to eat with such a person. The ninth scripture was 1 Corinthians 6:9. It was about how the unrighteous will not inherit the kingdom of God, including fornicators. The last scripture I remembered was Matthew 10:37. This stated He who loves father or mother more than ME (meaning Jesus) isn't worthy of ME. After all the scriptures were presented, read and explained, the Elders came to the conclusion I didn't display the correct attitude and therefore unrepentant. I didn't show any works that befitted repentance and felt my financial situation was more important than my spiritual. Brother James looked at me with an expression that said I should come clean with everything and maybe I would be spared. He wanted me to tell him what he already suspected, that I was forced into baptism from my mother. Then all the Elders closed their Bibles simultaneously. They said if I had anything else to comment on about the matter I should do so now. I thought long and hard. I really didn't have anything to say. In my mind, I wanted peace and closure, to finally move on no matter what their decision was. I said, "No, I have nothing to say." They stated that their position of being Elders was a very difficult one. They had to adhere to bible scriptures for reproving, correction and for discipline. It was not always an easy task but it had to be done in order to keep the congregation morally clean. Brother Ivory and Brother Badstone looked at Brother James for him to speak. What needed to be said finally came out. Brother James stood up and looked right at me. He was void of any facial expression. He said, "Danny, we have come to a unanimous decision that you will be **_expelled_** from the Christian Congregation of Jehovah's Witnesses, and no longer to have any association with Jehovah's Witnesses in good standing until you produce works or fruits that is befitting repentance and find it in your heart to return to being in Jehovah's favor. You are not allowed to participate in any Field Service activities and are restricted from commenting at the meetings." Brother James continued,"If you believe that a serious error in judgment has been made, and you wish to appeal the decision of this committee, you may do so by writing a letter clearly stating your reasons for an appeal. You have a week from today to do so. An appeal committee could again hear the case." He then asked if I understood what he just said and I told him that I did. Then Brother James said, "If you felt that I or Brother Ivory or Brother Badstone weren't fair in this decision, another committee can be arranged and that request must be in writing as well. If there isn't a written appeal received by next weekend, we take it that you won't be appealing our decision and an announcement will be made at the Kingdom Hall next Thursday night that you have been disfellowshipped. If you request to be reinstated, a written plea of reinstatement must be made to the body of Elders no matter what congregation you attend. You will have to go through us for recommendation." He had a smirk on his face, sounding like the King of all Elders when talking. I guess he wanted to let me know no matter what congregation I attended; there wouldn't be a loophole or a way of escaping them. I would always have to go through them because they were the original committee from where I was disfellowshipped. I didn't care. I don't remember if a prayer was said to conclude the meeting, I just remember leaving. Brother James dismissed me from his house like he would a dog. And then, it was all over. The double life was now single. There I was alone. I kept saying, "I'm disfellowshipped." and started thinking about what that really meant. I felt like I lost everything but couldn't really explain what I had lost. One part of me wanted to jump for joy. I wanted to yell and call all my Kingdom Hall peeps and tell them the good news. The other part of me wanted to hide somewhere. I was ashamed to be disfellowshipped. I didn't want to be seen by anyone again. I only knew a handful of people that were disfellowshipped. Just about all of them used to study the Bible with me at one point in time. I would to see them after they were disfellowshipped months or years later, and they sure didn't look well spiritually, mentally, physically and financially. They all had this lost look about them and they appeared confused about life. I wondered if I would become like them. *Will Jehovah put a curse on me so I would never be successful no matter what I did in life all because I'm disfellowshipped?* Without realizing it, I was letting this get the best of me. I definitely needed to get myself together. I received a call from my mother two weeks later, late Thursday night, after the Thursday night meeting was over. She said she received a call from several of her friends that still attended our old congregation. "They announced at the meeting tonight that you were disfellowshipped sweetie." There was a long pause from both of us before my mom started breaking down. She felt responsible for me being disfellowshipped and wished that she had listened to me about certain things that happened through out the 15 years of attending the Murdock Congregation. In my mind, she was responsible. I told my mother not to worry about it and I spoke briefly about what had happened when I met with the Elders. I told my mother the names of the Brothers that were on the committee and what kind of reactions I was getting from them. Out of no where she said, "Them damn Elders wanted me so bad, but instead of getting me, they disfellowshipped you. That damn residing Elder was the ring leader." She continued, "Now you see why I told you not to go to them damn Brothers from the Murdock Congregation? But you wouldn't listen! You thought your friend Brother James was sincere in helping you but you see now he wasn't sincere at all. And you trusted him! And where did it get you?" I retorted sharply, "It's a thing of the past and I wouldn't be disfellowshipped if I wasn't baptized, but that's another story." My mother yelled, "You're right, and I'm sorry. I felt I had no choice but to be hard on you. I didn't realize how much I pushed you." My mother and I talked for over two hours. She said to me, "Them damn Elders think they so smart and slick, telling you the only way back to the Hall is through them." She continued, "All they were trying to do was scare you, sweetie. You can always go to the Gretna Congregation here in Virginia and be reinstated in six months. You don't have to go through them." I told her to let it go. I confessed that being reinstated wasn't something I was interested at that moment, if ever. She laughed and said, "Don't worry, I still love you. You are still my son. This is only a minor setback. Those Elders from Murdock are going to get what's coming to them."

Chapter Seventeen: Life
After Disfellowshipped

The following month after I was disfellowshipped, I started to feel like an outcast as I continuously bumped into one Witness after another. The situations were awkward and frustrating and though I was excited about my newfound freedom, seeing people around put me right back into a box. I saw Sister Eugene from my old congregation in the supermarket in our area (Little Giant). She was walking through the aisle and saw me at a quick glance. She had her head down so I wouldn't be able to recognize her, but she couldn't keep it down forever. We collided at the checkout counter. I was standing in back of her at the checkout line. She saw me again, standing behind her; she smiled and quickly turned back around. It was awkward. And her inability to exchange words with me was just her following orders on how to treat a disfellowshipped Witness.

Some days later, in the same supermarket, I saw Brother Badstone, the Elder on the judicial committee that disfellowshipped me. He was in the dairy section of the store. He looked at me with a crazy look and I mirrored the same crazy expression back at him. We walked past each other without any words or gesture given. I wasn't going to hide from these Witnesses just because I wasn't in good standing with them. I made sure when I left my home that I was well groomed and my attire was sharp just to let them gossip among each other on how they saw me looking great and sharp as a tack. I knew they were gossiping because ... hey ... I did the same thing when I was with them. So, for that purpose, the last thing I wanted was to look like being disfellowshipped meant hitting hard times. That would give the entire congregation something to talk about. And trust me, they would talk.

The Witnesses would be saying, "Did you see Brother or Sister So-and-so? Oh-my-God! He or she looked horrible and lost so much weight. They must be doing drugs. That's what happens when you leave Jehovah."

It was amazing to me on how many Witnesses I saw after getting disfellowshipped. I didn't see any when I was living in the basement in my house, but as soon as I received "the D slip"; it was like I was being hunted down to feel ashamed by getting stares and the cold shoulder. I saw half the congregation on subways, buses, going and coming from work, or in the supermarket. I saw Sister Patti, the lady who "brought my mother in the truth" on the bus during morning rush hour. She just looked at me with a half smile and turned her head away. Every time a Witness saw me, I was always on point, my head up and smiling. The Witnesses I didn't care for never acknowledged me in passing and could care less of them speaking. They just looked at me and shook their heads trying to make me feel shameful. But, the Witnesses that used watch me while my mother was working just smiled when they saw me. They didn't speak, but when they saw me it was like a nod of approval to continue looking sharp and keeping my head up. My mother would call me and say, "Brother Ernie saw you on the bus looking good with your business suit on. He said you appeared in good spirits."

It took some years to get accustomed to being disfellowshipped. At first, I wasn't too fond of having the disfellowshipped label on me because I felt like I was judged as a spiritual failure to those who knew me. I felt like I couldn't get it together in anything I was doing. The organization made me feel like I was wrong and irresponsible and guilty of not getting my life straight with Jehovah.

I know now it was it was all a mind game, but that's how the organization does ones that have been disfellowshipped. They make you feel so shameful and worthless. They make you feel like the only way you can be happy in life again is to repent and come back. The only way you will be successful in life is having Jehovah God protecting you and associating with his wonderful organization. Everything else you attempt to do, you will fail because you not down with Jehovah and his organization no more. It's only a matter of time when depression hits, and some go back to the organization. As time went on, I snapped out of the self-pity and took it for what it was worth. Three men (imperfect men no less), did what they thought was right on the behalf of a manmade organization to discipline me. All of this overseen by the "governing body" filled with more imperfect men. This organization was made up and founded by imperfect men who had made mistakes just like me. They were not forthcoming about their mistakes', covering them up, which is documented all through their history. So I decided to reflect on what was important to God and not what was important to them. This didn't mean I would start doing it immediately, though. There is a saying: *"If you give someone enough rope, they will hang themselves."* I believe God does it the same way but no man knows the length of the rope. I figured to myself that God would allow me more time to figure him out after I figured myself out first. I started **not** caring about what the organization had labeled me and developed a self love about myself and as time went along, cutting out the middle man to God. That's how I was able to remain sane about what I had gone through … that is until my mother popped back up into the scene.

According to the organization, my mother and I were not allowed to have any association with each other. This meant no visits, no phone calls, no verbal or physical contact, no business dealings, and no spiritual talk. She had to shun me as well. She wasn't supposed to have any dealings with me, and I was kind of looking forward to it. I needed my mother to let go for a minute and let me do my thing. She was in Virginia and I was in New York. What I always wanted was my mother to be far away from me so I could enjoy a little FREEDOM! It was time to get my life together, to get an identity and no longer worry about an organization. The spiritual part of me was on hiatus. It was the perfect excuse for my mother not to have any more control over me, leaving me alone. It was a great thing to me. I still loved my mother and honored her just as the Bible states. I did right by her for far too long, allowing her to trick me into thinking I wouldn't be showing honor to her unless I got baptized. I thought I finally had some freedom, no longer under the influence of my mother. I thought the control she once had over me was finally gone. I couldn't conceive or think of how my mother would have another opportunity to take control over me again. She wasn't going to give up that easy, it didn't matter to her if I was disfellowshipped or not, she was determined to have me "Controlled" and have HER way with me.

My mother started visiting New York once a month to pick up money and associate with "the friends". Some of her girlfriends went to the Murdock congregation, however, she had plenty others that went to other congregations all over Queens. I had been disfellowshipped for four years. My life was like a rollercoaster ride. I was up, down, sideways, upside down, twists, turns, some good things happened along with some bad things but it was nothing I couldn't handle. The house I grew up in was lost in foreclosure. I was starting to become aware of some of my mother's other shady business dealings that affected me financially. The only thing that was able to repair my finances was time. I had the opportunity to open up for the rap group *Public Enemy* at a show when I lived in Virginia. I went to Toronto, Canada for a week to hang out with my homeboy Mikey D. My man Mikey D was the new emcee of the rap group, Main Source, replacing lead rapper Large Professor. We free styled and rhymed at some parties and had a great time. I won several rap contests that was sponsored by different production companies. One production company called *Black Cat Productions*, based out of Louisiana, flew to New York to present me with a $500.00 check for a rap contest they had on cable TV. I left New York several weeks later to record with them at one of the best recording studios in the Midwest. Paisley Park recording studios is in Minneapolis and is owned by the superstar pop singer Prince. I even saw the superstar himself in passing while I was there recording. I also met the P funk artist, George Clinton.

I stayed in Baton Rouge, Louisiana for three months, coming back to New York without a record deal again and lived in Harlem, Washington Heights, Downtown Brooklyn and Bed Stuy, Brooklyn. In late '93 my mother called me and said a woman she knew was renting a furnished apartment in East Elmhurst, Queens. She thought I should check it out. I did. The apartment was beautiful and cheap. But it was too good to be true. Why? It just so happen that my mother was included in the deal. She tricked me into thinking I was getting an apartment of my own. Since my credit was destroyed I thought maybe she was looking out for me. I realized my mother was part of the deal only after I signed the agreement. It was just another way for my mother to get back into controlling my life even though she was suppose to be shunning me because I was disfellowshipped. My mother never visited me when I lived in Manhattan or Brooklyn because I lived right in the hood and to her wasn't safe. As soon as I moved to East Elmhurst, Queens, here she comes visiting and eventually moved herself into my apartment, despite the fact that she already had a home in Virginia. I asked my mother, "Why are you here? Don't you have a home in Virginia?" She was coming up once a month from Virginia and not only was she coming up to stay with me, but I had to pick her up from the bus station as well. While she stayed with me, she would call her Jehovah's Witness friends and meet up with them. It didn't bother me at first because they all knew I was disfellowshipped and never came into the house. As time went on, my mother started getting a little more comfortable bringing her Jehovah Witness friends into my apartment. Her Jehovah Witness friends had no shame coming through, and neither did my mother. I used to come and walk into my apartment, to find a bunch of Jehovah's Witness Sisters sitting in my kitchen. They acted like the place was theirs, just chilling, and conversing with my mother like I was invisible. No one spoke a word to me. But they would give me funny looks at me like I shouldn't be there. These Witnesses had the audacity to stare me down in my own kitchen, trying to make me feel uncomfortable. Once, my mother suggested I go away from the kitchen while she had company and to take myself into the bedroom and stay there until her company left. She suggested that I do this every time her Witness friends came over, regardless of what I was doing in my own apartment. Fed up, I told my mother one day, "Maybe your Witness friends would like to see me in my birthday suit since I can't get to the bedroom without going through the kitchen." My mother looked at me and said, "Maybe I should smack the living day lights out of you," and laughed. I asked my mother, "How is it possible that you and your Witness friends can sit up in my apartment, talk, drink, laugh, with no care in the world that you're in the presence of someone that's disfellowshipped?" I thought you and "the friends" were supposed to be obedient and heed Bible counsel when it's giving through the organization, not be around me." I starting yelling at my mother, "You and them are a bunch of phonies sitting around here gossiping in an apartment that's being rented by a disfellowshipped individual. I thought I was supposed to be revolting to you, like a dog returning to its own vomit." My mother said, "Now sweetie, if there's one thing you remember in life, let this be it. My dedication and faith is to Jehovah and not men. Men will do anything to destroy your relationship with Jehovah, including men in the organization. You have to put your faith and trust in Jehovah, not men. Men will get you disfellowshipped. The faster you remember that, the faster you will see how serving Jehovah works over serving men." I looked at her and laughed, "I'll don't remember any men who forced me to get baptized either but I'll remember that for the future, if I decide to return to Jehovah". It's been 18 years since the last time I stepped into a Kingdom Hall. Sometimes on Thursday nights, around the time they would say the announcements, I used to think about what was being discussed and was I missing something. Maybe the organization had received some "new light" and predicting Armageddon again. I wonder what year they say Armageddon is going to be now. Will it be 2012 or before President Bush leaves office. Never less, my mother was trying to get me to go the memorial service in 1995. I told her, "I wasn't interested and don't ask me about going no where near a kingdom hall as long as I'm living." I had my sights on more important matters and could less about the organization, my mother, or anybody else that was a Jehovah Witness. It was time to move on and get a fresh start. I had been dating a friend I had met in March of 1995 and looking forward to being with her.

Five years had gone by since I was disfellowshipped and as the summer of 1995 approached, I had been planning for several months on leaving New York and decided to be with my lady friend and move to Albuquerque, New Mexico. My mother was pissed off at me because I told her a day before I left that I was moving. She wanted to know who was going to be paying the rent and utilities at the furnish apartment I was renting. I told her, "You can pay them since you live here." I already notified the owner of the home that I was moving and had not anticipated paying anything else after the month of July 1995. Her control of my life was finally over and I was looking forward to starting my new life in New Mexico. She was upset at me for several months but not too upset. My mother came to New Mexico in October of 1995 and attended my wedding. I guess me being disfellowshipped went right down the drain.

Over the years, my mother would mention to me about what was going on with some of the people still attending our old Murdock Avenue Congregation in Hollis, Queens, New York. My mother told me Brother Frank had died. Brother Andy was still single and trying to get into Bethel. Sister Bee's daughter married a white Elder from New Jersey. The residing Elder's daughter was still looking for anybody to marry. Sister Yolanda was still an undercover freak. And Brother Ross was getting married and moving to New Mexico. I interrupted my mother, "Brother Ross is getting married and moving where?" My mother said, "Brother Ross is moving to New Mexico." I found it extremely odd that someone I knew from my old congregation in New York would be moving 2000 miles across the country to Albuquerque, New Mexico within 15 minutes from me. I thought to myself, *what are the chances of me seeing this guy in New Mexico?* I wouldn't have believed it if Jehovah God himself had predicted it. Guess what? I ran dead smack into Brother Ross at a downtown Albuquerque, New Mexico tuxedo store.

I was living 35 miles south of the city of Albuquerque and working for the Department of Corrections for the State of New Mexico. My father-in-law was having a black tie affair at a nearby hotel in downtown Albuquerque that required me to rent a tuxedo for the evening. My father-in-law insisted I should go where he gets his tuxedos and to buy a tuxedo instead of renting one. He instructed me to go to the store, ask for the owner and tell the owner whom I was. I followed my father-in-law's instructions. The owner then hooked me up with my Tux's alterations. While there, I noticed five or six guys making their way into the tuxedo store. LO and BEHOLD, It was Brother Ross and his whole wedding party from my old congregation in Hollis, Queens, New York. When they saw me sitting at the table all the noise they were making turned into dead silence. They started mumbling with blank facial expressions, preparing themselves not to look at me. They tried their best not to look at me, but their eyes wandered towards me every-now-and-then. It was amusing. I figured they were wondering if I was getting a tuxedo for the same wedding. I was staring at them with a wide smirk. I joked with the owner of the store that I couldn't wait to wear my new tuxedo to this "wedding" I was invited to. I couldn't help but laugh to myself. We all looked stupid and awkward not talking to one another. Out of the five or six guys that were there, I watched three of them grow up in the Kingdom Hall. It was kind of weird not speaking or acknowledging each other. But that's how it is when you're a disfellowshipped Jehovah Witness. Having on Law Enforcement uniform confirmed to them I had no intentions of coming back to Jehovah. My disfellowshipped status was going to remain just that … disfellowshipped. After 30 or 40 minutes of waiting for the alterations to be done, my tuxedo was ready and I was ready to leave. I thanked the owner of the store for my tuxedo and walked out laughing to myself. It was the funniest and strangest thing that I ever imagine happening.

While working on the graveyard shift, I had plenty of time to think and write about everything that was bothering me since leaving the organization. What started, as writing in a notebook, was the beginning of this book. I had 10 sheets, back and front filled up, after the first night of writing. I couldn't wait to start my next night on the graveyard shift so I could finish. Writing was therapeutic. My soul spilled onto paper. When I finished, I had 50 pages of anger, bitterness and resentment built up inside me now free. I just couldn't take it anymore, as my writing was borderline bashing. Emotionally I was hurting far more than I imagined. I wanted to tell someone what I was going through and take a step forward on clearing this disfellowshipped matter with the organization, having my name cleared for once and for all. I built up the nerve to call the society at their world headquarters located in downtown Brooklyn, New York. I spoke to a Brother about my situation in brief. I stated to the Brother that I was forced into baptism and asked if there was something I could do to reverse my dedication and my baptism. The Brother's pause was so long I thought he hung up the phone. He said revoking my baptism couldn't be done. He assured me that my situation was different but nothing entirely new. The Brother stated he heard stories every day on how kids were forced into baptism and that they wanted their baptism status changed or reversed. He said that I was old enough to know right from wrong. "You were a grown man at 20 years old," he stated. "You knew what you wanted so you need to move on and stop blaming others and take responsibility for your own actions." He continued, "I'm tired of hearing excuses about young adults being forced into baptism, that they weren't ready yet. What you need to do is get back to Jehovah and be reinstated." I asked him, "How was I a man if I had been raised by a woman? What MEN in the organization stepped up to me and showed me how to be a man"? I asked again, "So, there isn't another way to resolve this"?" The Brother said sharply, "No! I'm sorry." I said, "Thank you for nothing." I was disappointed that we couldn't come to an agreement on anything. I knew writing a book would be a start on clearing this matter up. I would tell myself if the opportunity comes up to tell the world about my story, I would. I was thinking that I could receive some spiritual food from somewhere other than the Kingdom Hall. I haven't claimed any particular religion but have listened to some religions programs on TV like Pastor Frederick Price, based out of Los Angeles, California. I've listened to T.D. Jakes from Dallas, Texas. Since I've been living in Atlanta, I visited New Birth Church in Lithonia, Georgia where Bishop Eddie Long is the Senior Pastor. I've attended Hopewell Church in Norcross with Pastor William Shoal and New Mercies Church in Lilburn, Georgia where Pastor Jesse Curney is the Senior Pastor. I had the opportunity to visit my cousin's church in Barstow, California while on vacation. That was an inspiring moment because I hadn't seen my first cousin in over 30 years. I enjoyed the services at their church. I must say that my first visit to a church as an adult was the weirdest feeling for me. I didn't know if I should clap, sing, dance, jump up and down, and dive to the floor or what. I really didn't know how to react because going to the Kingdom Hall was the complete opposite of a church. I remember the first time I went to New Birth at its old location in Lithonia in the winter. It was dark outside and service was at 6:00 AM. It was packed! There were law enforcement directing traffic and cars everywhere. I couldn't believe I was going to a church of this magnitude and it seem unreal to me. I couldn't help noticing all the women I was seeing in church. It felt like I was attending a spiritual disco. I wish I could have had a mixture of each pastor I'd heard speak, and have it all combined like a spiritual gumbo. My opinion of religion went up and down like the weather because there are hundreds of pastors, reverends, and priests that sound appealing and sound sincere and are great speakers. But all of them take a scripture or several scriptures out of the Bible and expound them into what they think it means. After what I went through as a Jehovah Witness, I'd rather bypass religion altogether. I'll take my chances going straight to God until He tells me or shows me something different. Until then, I will continue searching and seeking a righteous and spiritual path that's goes along with what the bible says. Even then, I still will ask questions.

My first time voting was six years ago and I had no clue on what I was doing in the voting booth. I didn't know how to operate the voting machine and didn't know the backgrounds of any of the candidates. I find myself sometimes having verbal spats with people with different religious backgrounds. I debate with them like I'm still a Jehovah Witness. It's a constant battle within to rid myself of the Doctrine I once represented. After all, this is all I knew. The organization discourages their publishers to be Independent in their thinking when it comes to researching and examining scriptures for themselves. That's how the organization keeps CONTROL. I feel like if my spiritually is on the line, I will continue to ask, study, search, and investigate as much as I can. Don't read me scriptures no more, EXPLAIN them! I will not be CONTROLLED again. I know the day has to come where I need to return off my spiritual vacation and be responsible for my family and my spirituality. God will hold me accountable. I just don't know when or how I will go about doing that. One thing is for sure the possibilities of returning to the Kingdom Hall are none. I have learned not to say 'never' but I don't see it happening. When I was in New York some months ago, I was driving on Hollis Avenue and passed an empty building on where the Kingdom Hall was and wondered where it disappeared. I drove another block or two and saw the new Kingdom Hall, which is now located on 199th Street and Hollis Avenue. It was huge! I slowed down the car and pulled over for a couple of minutes, staring at it for a while. I thought about all the memories I had of attending the Kingdom Hall, hanging out on Hollis Avenue and 201st Street, rapping on the corner of the Kingdom Hall after the meetings. I reflected on how I used to dress and associate with "the friends". I started the car back up, took one last look at the new Kingdom Hall and smiled. I said to myself that I have no regrets on how my life turned out. I pulled off from the parking spot and drove off slowly as the raindrops were getting heavy. As I drove past the kingdom hall, I was hoping to see someone I knew in the front of the kingdom hall so they can see me and run back inside and tell him or her they saw me. That was one of the happiest moments in my life. I haven't smiled that hard since that day. It's been 19 years since I walked away from that kingdom hall and it has been 16 years since I was disfellowshipped. It's now the Present day. It's now me and my family and I never thought I would be free. Finally I can say... The Kingdom Hall is No More!

BIBLIOGRAPHY

Awake magazine 5/22/1969 page 15

Watchtower magazine 10/15/1969 pages 622, 623

Watchtower magazine 7/15/1967 pages 446-447

Watchtower magazine 5/1/1968 page 272

Watchtower magazine 10/15/1966 page 631

The Kingdom Ministry May 1974 page 3

Watchtower magazine 7/15/1976 pages 440-441

Watchtower magazine 5/15/1922

Millions now living will never die pages 89-90

JWfiles.com – Shawn Research web site

The Holy Bible (NKJV) New King James Version – Thomas Nelson

The New World Translation of the Holy Scriptures

Watchtower Bible

Tract Society of New York, - 1961

Printed in the United States
124545LV00003B/16/P